3-MINUTE **J.R.R.TOLKIEN**

3-MINUTE
J.R.R. TOLKIEN

An unauthorized biography
of the world's most revered
fantasy writer

Gary Raymond
Foreword by **John Howe**

METRO BOOKS
New York

METRO BOOKS
New York

An Imprint of Sterling Publishing
387 Park Avenue South
New York, NY 10016

This book was conceived,
designed, and produced by
Ivy Press
210 High Street, Lewes,
East Sussex BN7 2NS, UK
www.ivypress.co.uk

CREATIVE DIRECTOR Peter Bridgewater
PUBLISHER Jason Hook
EDITORIAL DIRECTOR Caroline Earle
ART DIRECTOR Michael Whitehead
DESIGNER Glyn Bridgewater
PROJECT EDITOR Jamie Pumfrey

ISBN 978-1-4351-4522-1

For information about custom editions,
special sales, and premium and corporate
purchases, please contact Sterling
Special Sales at 800-805-5489 or
specialsales@sterlingpublishing.com

Manufactured in China

2 4 6 8 10 9 7 5 3 1

www.sterlingpublishing.com

Contents

Foreword

Myth-making for the modern man
by John Howe

Clearly, we humans need myths. Every age of humanity has created them, to recount and to remind us of those things that carry meanings so crucial to our survival as a species. But, as we progress, we leave myths by the wayside and we find others that contain new versions of the truths we require. In our scientific age we no longer "believe" in myths, we have other explanations that suffice. Science and technology, reason and psychology; we have many explanations and much knowledge to tell us who and where we are in the universe.

But we still carry myths with us. We create them ceaselessly—from Dryden's noble savages to last week's urban legends. Ideologies are mythologized, we bust myths, we refute them, we dissect and collate them, we consign them to scholarly seminars and children's books. We conscientiously display them, as truthful "untruths," in the non-fiction section of our libraries.

Mythical tales are never untruthful. They reflect the irrepressible desire for things as they *should* be, they are stories that allow us to be reconciled with the human condition, with death, with our forever-lost origins and other unanswered questions. (Science and religion adamantly provide explanations, but they demand the rejection or qualification of other answers.)

But we don't *tell* myths any more. We feel we've grown out of them in a way, and that meaning must be explicit to be understood. Naturally, we are wrong, because the "truth" of myth is never signposted. It is cloaked and encrypted in symbol and allegory, it is linked to etymology and history, it is not an itemized set of reminders or a simple cautionary tale.

A century ago, T. E. Hulme qualified Romanticism as "spilt religion." Today, he might well have said the same of modern fantasy and our appetite for it. Much fantasy is more form than substance, but occasionally an author redefines the genre with an enduring and personal revisiting of those themes that have been ever-present in myths since they began being told.

Myths are stories from which time has stripped much meaning. If we are dutiful readers, we know the symbolism of each character, who personifies the seasons, how earth-diving creation myths came about, which pagan gods have become saints. We can follow the threads from culture to culture, but while this does inform us, it does not necessarily take us on a journey. But it is undoubtedly on a journey through myth that J. R. R. Tolkien invites us. The underlying density of his tales is built on those things he did *not* invent but which he spent a lifetime diligently mapping. And, as with all true myths, in Tolkien's tales we are caught up in the story, swept along by the narrative, and reach the end with the odd sentiment that we have *understood* something, although we cannot put our fingers on it. And nor should we.

Our grasp of the *meaning* of Middle-earth should be intuitive, as instinctive as the author's need to weave meanings into his narrative. But our connection with the mythology of this fantasy landscape need not stop there. Tolkien's work can be seen as an open door into an invigorating and eternally relevant world vision; it can help us understand the worlds of those who created the myth cycles we all know in their far drier and more scholarly or comparative forms, to bring them alive through his conviction and energy, to make them magic again. Tolkien invites us to imagine being swept away in the depth and breadth of a telling and to blink at the sudden *making of sense* that has come unawares.

Enchantment is not simply entertainment, it is an opportunity for deeper understanding of the world and humanity's place in it.

We need myths. We would do well to listen attentively when they are told so well.

Jo Howe

August 21, 2012,
Wellington, New Zealand

How the Book Works

This book tells the story of J. R. R. Tolkien in three parts. The first chapter explores Tolkien's life, narrating how a childhood talent for learning languages and inventing new ones, and a love for the countryside of his youth, were forged in the furnace of the First World War into a creative force that found expression in the imagined landscape of Middle-earth. The literature and mythology with which Tolkien described and developed this fantasy world are the subjects of the second chapter. It considers *The Hobbit* and *The Lord of the Rings* alongside lesser-known work, academic achievements, and significant books such as *The Silmarillion*. The final chapter describes Tolkien's influence and the almost magical spell that his writing continues to cast over popular culture, from literature and art to computer games and music; and, of course, the movies that have led a whole new audience to join the Tolkien fellowship.

Chapter 1

Life

Chapter 2

Works

Chapter 3

Influence

3-minute J. R. R. Tolkien

Each chapter of this book is made up of twenty 3-minute features. So, in the Works chapter you will find separate features on The Two Towers, *magic and religion, and Middle-earth. Every feature has three paragraphs, each dealing with one aspect of the main topic. For example, the feature on Magic and Religion (below) has paragraphs on "the nature of evil" (linking the character of Sauron to Catholic theology); "magical powers" (considering the role of sorcery within the Middle-earth mythology); and "religion, gods, and wizards" (assessing the faiths of Tolkien's imagined races). A single paragraph will take you about one minute to digest, meaning that each feature can be understood in about three minutes. So, 3-minute J. R. R. Tolkien!*

Chapter 2 Works

Magic and Religion

WILLOW

KRULL

The nature of evil
In Tolkien's Middle-earth, "evil" is a complex notion and is not, as some may suggest, symbolized by cipher characters and shadows of **pathetic fallacy**. Sauron, as the greatest example of Tolkien's idea of evil, has a long, turbulent, and varied personal history that stretches out to the beginning of the Middle-earth's creation. A **corrupted celestial warrior**, his journey reflects in many ways that of the angel Lucifer in Christian mythology or, more accurately, a disciple of Lucifer, making Morgoth the devil himself. Sauron was once just, and his journey to becoming the Dark Lord of Mordor is often defined by an absence of good, a particularly **Catholic theological idea**. Much that informs Tolkien's weightier themes came from such tightly held Catholic beliefs.

Magical powers
Although magic exists in the realms of Middle-earth, Tolkien is careful not to rely on it heavily either as a device to deliver dramatic tension or as a deus ex machina. Importantly, not just anyone can **obtain magical powers**—mostly, those with inherent powers are not originally born of Middle-earth. The wizards are celestial, as are the origins of the Elves and Sauron himself. Most other magic is imparted from these **"angelic" figures** who have a direct connection to the creators through spells and powerful items such as the Ring. Thus magic is not a **pagan power**, and neither is it a truly fantastical whim, but rather it has a definite connection to the Old Testament "magic" of Christianity's celestial powers.

Religion, gods, and wizards
Religion and faith are important to the peoples of Middle-earth, although it takes many forms. Many races have quasi-pagan beliefs, such as the druidic, agricultural forces in elven and dwarvish faith systems who see the presence of a **supreme power** not in cathedrals but in the earth itself. In the histories of Middle-earth, Tolkien lays out the creation and evolutionary myths that are the fabric of much organized religion. The wizards are certainly **representative of angels**, and like the angels of Christian mythology come in a variety of shapes and sizes. Indeed, it is Gandalf and Saruman who offer the closest things Middle-earth has to a gnostic theological strand, as **"gods" who have taken an earthly form.**

3-second Quest
As important as religion and faith were to J. R. R. Tolkien, it is only the careful reader who can identify strands of his Catholicism in his fiction.

Related Thoughts
see also
THE SCHOOL YEARS
page 24
MYTHOLOGY
page 90

❝I don't feel under any obligation to make my story fit with formalized Christian theology, though I actually intended it to be consonant with Christian thought and belief.❞

92

Instant expert

The structure of the book means that each of the three chapters will take about an hour to digest and that the whole book will furnish you with a solid understanding of the life history, literary highlights, and importance of J. R. R. Tolkien in about three hours. In addition to all that, each chapter concludes with a timeline and glossary to help you keep your thoughts in order. You'll have to read Tolkien's own works to fully appreciate and enjoy his genius, but this is the quickest way to discover the man behind the magic and the real-world experiences that helped shape the most fully realized fantasy landscape in literature.

Tolkien's World

J. R. R. Tolkien is a unique literary figure. He created not merely works of fiction but a world, Middle-earth, that mirrors and shines a light upon the wonders of our own. Critics were at first divided by Tolkien's classic works, *The Hobbit* (George Allen & Unwin, 1937) and the trilogy *The Lord of the Rings*—*The Fellowship of the Ring* (1954), *The Two Towers* (1954), and *The Return of the King* (1955). The reading public, however, were quick to appreciate their worth. *The Lord of the Rings* has become one of the bestselling books of all time, and Middle-earth continues to spin at the center of fantasy literature, art, music, virtual worlds, and Oscar-winning movies. Its creation can be traced back to Tolkien's less known work. As Merton Professor of English Language and Literature at Oxford, he explored Anglo-Saxon and Norse sagas and poems, building an understanding of the significance of myth and a vocabulary of its essential elements. His scholarship equipped him to imagine a world intricately mapped with its own geography, bound together with its own intertwined mythology and language. As the student became the master, Tolkien wove his own myths, so convincing that they endure perhaps more strongly than the ancient tales. In 1936, Tolkien gave an influential lecture, *Beowulf, The Monsters and The Critics*, identifying the power of the Anglo-Saxon poem and defending its dragons and other beasts. He might instead have been speaking of his own work when he said: "It glimpses the cosmic and moves with the thought of all men concerning the fate of human life and efforts."

Scandinavian Dragons

Tolkien had strong links to Scandinavia through his studies of Norse and Anglo-Saxon myth, saga, and poetry. His 1936 lecture Beowulf: The Monsters and the Critics *remains a defining study of* Beowulf, *the ancient poem about dragon-slaying in Scandinavia.*

Battlefields of France

Experiencing the horrors of the Battle of the Somme in 1916, Tolkien suffered illness and the loss of most of his closest friends in the Great War, and echoes of the battlefield resound in the Dead Marshes of Middle-earth.

1433 P. 2 - VISPBACH MIT MATTERHORN

Adventures in Switzerland

Inspired by a hiking holiday in the snowy landscape of the Swiss Alps in the summer of 1911, when he was 19 years old, Tolkien later noted how it had inspired The Hobbit, *and Bilbo Baggins' journey through the Misty Mountains.*

Mountains of South Africa

Although he left South Africa when he was three, the dramatic landscape of the suitably named Drakensberg (Dragon) Mountains provided a dramatic backdrop for Tolkien's earliest memories.

Tolkien's Landscape

Studies in Leeds

As Professor of English at the University of Leeds 1920 to 1925, Tolkien explored philology and mythology in what became one of the best English departments in the country, working on a classic edition of Sir Gawain and the Green Knight.

Sarehole Mill

From the age of four, Tolkien lived near Birmingham in the shadow of the 16th-century Sarehole Mill, the inspiration for the Great Mill of The Hobbit. *He played in farmland that evoked the unspoilt Shire and imbued Tolkien with a lifelong love of nature and the countryside.*

Oxford Home

Tolkien spent much of his life and career in Oxford, where he found likeminded friends, the ideal place to pursue his studies, and the woodland landscape that offered both the essential promise of long walks and an ideal model for Middle-earth.

Seaside Retreat

Having cherished the weekend breaks with his family in Bournemouth for many years, Ronald and Edith made their home by the sea in 1968. With Tolkien's growing fame invading life in Oxford, the south coast allowed Ronald and Edith to fully enjoy their time together.

13

A Modern Mythology

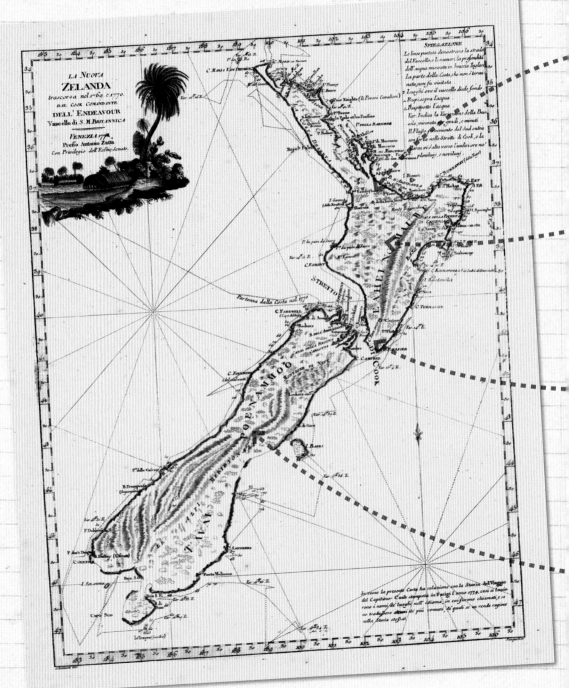

Hobbiton

For the movie versions of The Lord of the Rings *and* The Hobbit, *director Peter Jackson's New Zealand homeland provided the perfect diverse blend of idyllic countryside and foreboding mountains. The army helped to create "Hobbiton," digging thirty-seven hobbit holes near Matamata to evoke the Shire.*

Mount Doom

It took a combination of two active volcanoes, Mount Ngauruhoe and Mount Ruapehu in Tongariro National Park, to capture the spirit of Mount Doom, where the One Ring was forged and where it must be destroyed.

Minas Tirith

The fortress city of Minas Tirith, capital of Gondor, and the valley of Helm's Deep, where the climactic battle takes place, were built at Dry Creek Quarry, a vast mining complex at the bottom of Haywards Hill in Wellington.

Edoras

Edoras, capital city of Rohan, where Aragorn and Gandalf meet with King Théoden, was built in the spectacular Rangitata Valley beneath Mount Sunday, a setting eminently worthy of the drama of Middle-earth.

Tolkien's Works

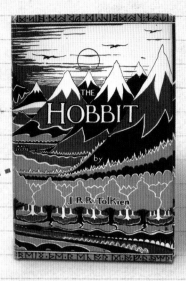

The Hobbit

Published September 21, 1937, by George Allen &
Unwin, 310 pages, the book was an instant success
and established Tolkien as a successful author. It
was nominated for the Carnegie Medal and awarded
a prize from the New York Herald Tribune for
best juvenile fiction.

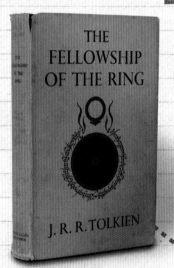

The Fellowship of the Ring

Published July 24, 1954, by George Allen & Unwin,
531 pages, this was the first of the three volumes of
The Lord of the Rings. *Tolkien had originally*
hoped to publish the novel in one volume, but it
was structured in six parts, and this book comprised
"The Ring Sets Out" and "The Ring Goes South."

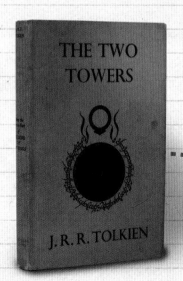

The Two Towers

Published November 11, 1954, by George Allen &
Unwin, 416 pages, the second part of the trilogy
encompassed "The Treason of Isengard" and
"The Ring Goes East."

Other Works

Tolkien's other works included The Adventures of Tom Bombadil, *published in 1962 by George Allen & Unwin;* Farmer Giles of Ham, *written in 1937 and published in 1949; and* Smith of Wootton Major, *published in 1967.*

The Silmarillion

Published in 1977 by George Allen & Unwin, 365 pages, this work was developed, edited, and published by Tolkien's son Christopher. Originally offered for publication before The Lord of the Rings, *it sets out in depth the mythology of the universe with Middle-earth at its heart.*

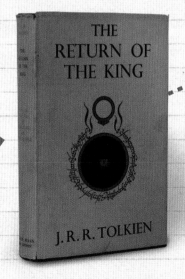

The Return of the King

Published October 20, 1955, by George Allen & Unwin, 624 pages, the conclusion of the epic tale narrates "The War of the Ring" and "The End of the Third Age." Tolkien felt the chosen title revealed too much of the story, and would have preferred "The War of the Ring" as the name of the book.

Chapter 1

Life

The Journey Begins

Birth

On January 3, 1892, in the wide expanses of South Africa's Orange Free State Province, John Ronald Reuel was born to Arthur and Mabel Tolkien. The Tolkiens had moved to **Bloemfontein** from England in 1890, where Arthur was a bank manager. Thinking that the South African climate would be detrimental to her young sons' health, in 1894 she returned with them to **Birmingham**. Shortly after, Arthur, who had stayed in Bloemfontein on business, died from a fever. Although John Ronald Reuel (or Ronald as he was now known) experienced his land of birth only briefly and at the earliest stage of his life, some believe that the harsh landscape and perilous wildlife (particularly his encounter with a **large baboon spider**) remained with him and informed some famous sequences and characters in his work.

The family name

The Tolkien name is believed to have derived from Lower Saxony. Several theories exist regarding the meaning of the name, but the most interesting is that it comes from the German word **tollkühn**, meaning "foolhardy." Since their arrival in England in the eighteenth century, members of the Tolkien family had always been craftsmen, and their name had been **well respected** in many skills in Birmingham for generations. Ronald's grandfather, John Benjamin Tolkien, had continued his family's artistic inclinations as a piano teacher and tuner, and as a music seller. Arthur Reuel, however, saw a steadier line of work in banking. Ronald would have a number of childhood homes dotted around the Birmingham map.

A new path

Mabel's family, the Suffields, had for generations run successful businesses, including a hosiers and a stationers, from Lamb House in Birmingham. By the time that Mabel Tolkien returned to England with her two children, Ronald and his younger **brother Hilary**, in 1895, the Tolkiens, several generations out of Lower Saxony and despite a few years in South Africa, were well and truly anglicized. Some years after Arthur's death, living life on the genteel side of poverty, Mabel Tolkien, to the chastisement and financial ostracism of her Baptist family, was ordained into the **Roman Catholic Church**. This Catholicism was to shape Ronald's thinking throughout his life and encased the morality of his written work and the worlds in which his characters dwelled.

3-Second Quest

J. R. R. Tolkien was born in 1892. This was the same year that Arthur Conan Doyle published *The Adventures of Sherlock Holmes* and Russia began constructing the Trans-Siberian Railway.

Related Thoughts

see also
CHILDHOOD
page 22
MAGIC AND RELIGION
page 92

❝I am a West-Midlander by blood and took to early West-Midland Middle English as to a known tongue as soon as I set my eyes on it.❞
THE LETTERS OF J.R.R. TOLKIEN

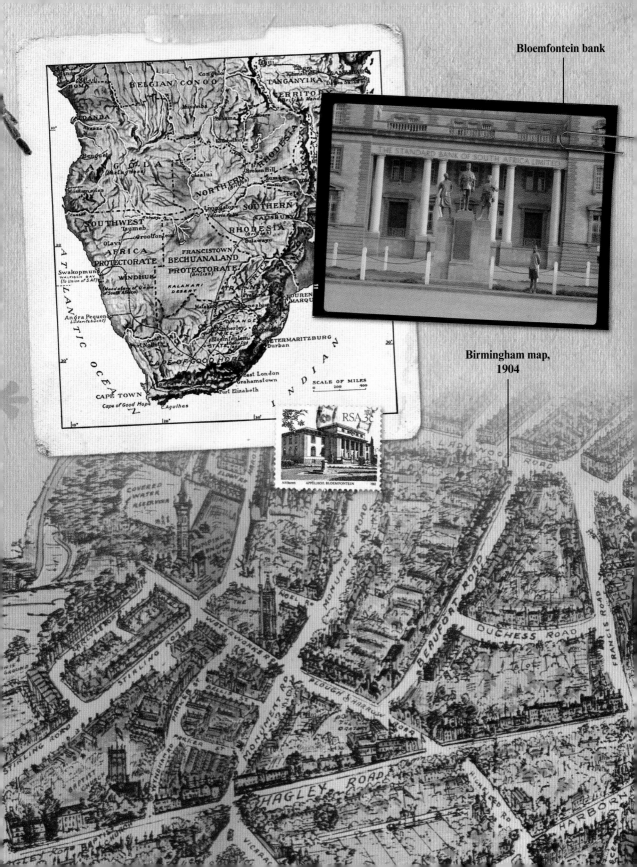

Bloemfontein bank

Birmingham map, 1904

Childhood

Home schooling

Now settled back in England, Mabel schooled her two sons herself, and Ronald became a keen pupil and avid reader. His mother introduced him to **botany**, and he took to sketching rural scenes and images of plants and trees. But the subject that inspired him the most at this early age was **languages**. Mabel taught him rudimentary Latin, which he grasped with startling ease and proficiency. Ronald later stated how he had disliked *Treasure Island* and found *Alice in Wonderland* "deeply disturbing." Rather, it was the fantasy novels of the minister **George MacDonald** and the fairy tales of Scottish scholar Andrew Lang that proved to have the most significant literary impact on the young Tolkien.

Nature versus industry

In 1896 Mabel relocated the family to the scenic hamlet of **Sarehole**, a place that was to have a permanent effect on Ronald's outlook. There he met a certain Dr. Gamgee and spent the summer walking in the countryside and picking flowers. When Ronald gained entry to school in Birmingham in 1900, the Tolkiens reluctantly moved back to the city. Tolkien, the **young linguist**, was mesmerized by the exotic names on the coal trains that passed their lodgings—names such as Nantyglo, Penrhiwceiber, and Senghenydd—as they rumbled toward the Welsh mining towns. In these early years, Tolkien was in close quarters to **contrasting landscapes**—dark, satanic mills alongside the green and pleasant land of the shires of England. The industrialization of the countryside would become a lifelong preoccupation.

Orphaned

After the schism in the Tolkien family in the wake of Mabel's conversion to Roman Catholicism, Mabel and the boys found themselves often close to destitution. Then, on November 4, 1904, at the age of 34, Mable succumbed to type 1 diabetes, almost two decades before the discovery of insulin. Orphaned and without the support of the Baptist Tolkiens, Ronald, aged 12, and Hilary, aged 10, were taken in by **Father Francis Xavier Morgan** of the Birmingham Oratory and spent the rest of their childhoods in the Edgbaston area of Birmingham. They lived in the shadow of **Perrott's Folly** and the tower of the **Edgbaston Waterworks**—two prominent edifices all the more striking for their similarity to the two towers that appeared in Tolkien's *The Lord of the Rings* many decades later.

3-Second Quest
After the death of his father, Tolkien's mother introduced him to several subjects, most notably languages, that would become a defining element of his entire life.

Related Thoughts
see also
THE JOURNEY BEGINS
page 20
CONSERVATION AND
LANDSCAPE
page 148

❝ My mother pointed out to me that I could not say 'a green great dragon,' but had to say 'a great green dragon.' I wondered why and still do. ❞

*THE LETTERS OF
J.R.R. TOLKIEN*

George MacDonald

Edgbaston Waterworks

Perrott's Folly

School Years

An academic in the making

In the aftermath of their mother's death, Ronald and Hilary, under the financial and spiritual guidance of the warm and kindly **Father Francis**, were given board and lodging by their Aunt Beatrice. Unfortunately, the house was a drab environment and Beatrice a rather distant presence, and so Ronald and Hilary spent much of their time serving at the Oratory while also immersing themselves in their studies at **King Edward's School**. Ronald, in particular, excelled. He came top of the class and built on his early interest and aptitude for languages to show true academic potential. The school, as well as the Oratory, became the true home of the young Tolkien, who would go on to be a lifelong academic and devout Catholic.

Discovering legends

Under the watchful eye of King Edward's headmaster, the brilliant and eccentric classicist and inventor **Robert Cray Gilson**, Tolkien was encouraged not just to study and understand Latin, Greek, French, and German but to delve much deeper into the **bones of the languages**. Tolkien began studying their origins and the strands that bonded them together across geography and time. Now he also began to be taught by schoolmaster George Brewerton who turned Tolkien first on to studies in Anglo-Saxon and then on to the texts of **Beowulf**, the Arthurian legends, and the adventures of valiant heroes—in particular, the story of *Sir Gawain and the Green Knight*.

The language inventor

Like many boys of his age, Ronald began to devise new words that soon developed into his own language. The difference with Tolkien's invention, however, was that it came from the viewpoint of a **philologist's expertise**. It was recognized early on—as Mabel had predicted—that Ronald was not only blessed with a true academic ability (despite an unusually rapid speaking style) but his **study of language** was beyond mere academia and was in fact a deep and passionate love for the shape, sound, and composition of words in all their forms. Under the galvanizing enthusiasm of his schoolmasters, the **young Tolkien** was set on his path to becoming one of the most eminent philologists of his time.

3-Second Quest
Tolkien was lucky enough to encounter teachers at King Edward's School who identified the boy's academic ability and nurtured his passion for languages.

Related Thoughts
see also
STUDYING MYTHS
page 32
TEACHER AND SCHOLAR
page 40

❝ *I wish life was not so short... Languages take such a time and so do all the things one wishes to know about.* **❞**
THE LOST ROAD

King Edward's School,
Birmingham

J. R. R. Tolkien
at school

King Edward's
schoolmasters

First Verse

A kindred spirit

In 1908 Father Francis began to look for a more comfortable environment in which the boys could spend their teenage years. He found spare rooms at the home of friends of the Oratory, a **Mr. and Mrs. Faulkner**. It was here, aged 16, that Ronald struck up a close friendship with another of the Faulkners' lodgers—the young and beautiful **Edith Bratt**. She was also an orphan and three years his senior. Ronald and Edith found in each other kindred spirits in experience, if not in academic pursuits, Edith having had a limited education. It was not long before this friendship grew deeper with Ronald and Edith **declaring their love** for each other in 1909.

Biding time

Ronald and Edith conducted a romance that constituted long walks, conversations that went deep into the night, and memories of **watching the sun come up** over the rooftops from the windows of the Faulkners' house. But gossip was a popular pastime in such small neighborhoods, and Father Francis, who was like a father to the Tolkien boys, soon found out about the goings-on. Deeply concerned that Ronald was romantically entwined with an older girl who was living under the same roof, Father Francis **forbade him** from seeing or even writing to Edith until he was 21. Recognizing he owed everything to the kindness of his guardian, Ronald, grim with depression, obeyed Father Francis' wishes.

The Barrovian Society

During this time, Ronald and a small clique of school friends at King Edward's began meeting regularly at the tearooms and then at the **Barrow Stores café**. They named themselves first the Tea Club and then the Barrovian Society, soon becoming known by the combined acronym, T.C.B.S. It was under the influence of this group of young intellectuals that Ronald wrote his first creative pieces. In the main he penned some **unremarkable poetry**, but it showed some significant influences in light of what he was to go on to write. In 1910 he watched J. M. Barrie's play **Peter Pan** at the Birmingham Theatre. He recognized immediately that it had a profound effect on him, but, interestingly, he seemed at the same time aware that the effect would not only be deep but long-lasting.

3-Second Quest
Tolkien began to adjust to thoughts that writing could be as important to him as reading, composing poems influenced by the books he was exposed to.

Related Thoughts
see also
THE INKLINGS
page 42
OXFORD LIFE
page 44

❝ *The realm of fairy-story is wide and deep and high and filled with many things.* **❞**
ON FAIRY STORIES

Barrow's Store café, c. 1905

Peter Pan

Adventures and Sagas

The scholarship secured

In 1910, at the second attempt, Ronald passed his scholarship exams, which gained him entrance to **Oxford University** to read Classics. As the first Tolkien to go to university, Ronald was determined to be a successful academic, and he began exhibiting his considerable gifts in his areas of interest. While still at King Edward's, his future secure, he delivered a lecture on the **Norse sagas** to the literature society, impressing many by reading his examples in the original tongue. He also discovered the **Finnish folktales of the *Kalevala*** and was immediately engrossed by the characters and stories, and the tapestry of the myths therein. The young Tolkien had found a world of fantasy and magic in which he felt completely at home.

A mountain expedition

In the summer between leaving King Edward's and attending Oxford, Ronald and Hilary were taken as members of a party, organized by friends of the Oratory, on a walking holiday to the **Swiss Alps**. On the trip they spent much time hauling great packs through mountain passes, sleeping rough in haylofts or barns, and visiting strange villages thousands of feet up at the foot of the **Aletsch glacier**. The journey was remembered by Tolkien as one fraught with dangers, such as tumbling ice balls and deep crevasses, and filled with encounters with strange peoples—from eccentric local guides to wealthy French ladies—all of which took place in a long journey through the dazzling whiteness and black shadows of the **Matterhorn**.

Gandalf makes his appearance

Besides the whiff of danger and adventure amid the eternally **dramatic landscapes** of the Swiss Alps, Tolkien took something else from his trip that was sure to influence the worlds and peoples he would one day create in his stories. Before his return to England, Ronald purchased a gift box of some picture postcards. In this box were cards displaying some of the artwork of the German painter J. Madlener. Included was a reproduction of Madlener's painting ***Der Berggeist***, or "mountain spirit." The spirit is an old man in a robe with a long beard and pointed hat. He sits upon a rock in a woodland with snowcapped mountains in the background and a fawn nuzzling into his hand. Many years later, Tolkien wrote across the postcard the words: "**Origin of Gandalf**."

3-Second Quest

Thinking back to the Swiss walking holiday, Tolkien would often remark (echoing the words of Bilbo Baggins in *The Fellowship of the Ring*) that he would one day like to see the mountains again.

Related Thoughts

see also
STUDYING MYTHS
page 32
MIDDLE EARTH
page 94

❝ *All we have to decide is what to do with the time that is given us.* **❞**
THE FELLOWSHIP OF THE RING

Aletsch glacier

Oxford

Home from home

For Tolkien, the halls of **Exeter College, Oxford**, were his first real home since the death of his mother. Oxford University in 1911 was populated almost entirely by the children of the upper classes, and the small contingency of students who made it to the hallowed cloisters on **academic scholarships** were often the victims of snobbery. Luckily for Tolkien, however, Exeter—one of the more unfashionable colleges at the time—did not have such traditions of division, and he soon settled in and made good friends. He threw himself into clubs and societies, playing rugby well, joining the debating team and Essay Club, and establishing a close-knit group of young intellectuals similar in many ways to the T.C.B.S. It was called the **Apolausticks**—"those devoted to self-indulgence."

Discovering talents

During his first year at Oxford, Tolkien began to lose interest in the works of the Greek and Latin poets and philosophers, and he moved toward **Germanic literature**. He was spending more time developing his own invented languages than he was in attending lectures on philosophers and playwrights such as **Seneca and Aristophanes**. Using his specialist subject of Comparative Philology as a springboard, Tolkien began to explore previously murky linguistic waters. Under the guidance of the famous philologist Professor Joseph Wright, Tolkien focused his studies on the Gothic language and grew a deep, poetic love for the language of the Welsh. He awakened his childhood talent for sketching and studied **calligraphy** with great success.

The reunion

On the very evening of his **21st birthday**, Ronald, dizzy with excitement, wrote his first words to Edith Bratt in three years in the hope of rekindling their romance after the imposed isolation from one another. To Ronald's distress, she replied that she had become engaged. Showing much of his **determined character**, Tolkien boarded a train to Cheltenham, where Edith had lived for the last three years. He asked her to marry him, and she said "Yes," claiming that she had thought he had forgotten her. Although they did not marry for some years yet, and they had grown to be very different people from when they had last known each other, they happily **reaffirmed their love**.

3-Second Quest
Tolkien, having never truly settled in any of his lodgings after the death of his mother, found a family-of-sorts and a welcoming environment in the hallowed halls of Oxford academe.

Related Thoughts
see also
FIRST VERSE
page 26
OXFORD LIFE
page 44

[On Edith]
" *Her hair was raven, her skin clear, her eyes bright, and she could sing and dance.* **"**

THE LETTERS OF J.R.R. TOLKIEN

Exeter College,
Oxford

Studying Myths

Middle-earth

Ronald found that he was unsuited to the study of subjects about which he was not deeply passionate. In time, his classics work was supplanted by his extra-curricular love affair with **medieval languages**. After scraping a Second Class Degree in 1913, Tolkien was convinced by Exeter College's English department, who spent much energy on Anglo-Saxon and Scandinavian languages and who had spotted his faultless comparative philology paper, to join their program for his postgraduate studies. It was now that he was introduced to the study and **mythologies of Old Icelandic**, such as the *Völuspà* or "Prophecy of the Seeress" preserved in the *Poetic Edda*. He also studied the religious **Anglo-Saxon poems of Cynewulf**, and it was in his Crist that Tolkien first encountered the term "Middle-earth."

Oxford gent

In June 1913, Edith moved to the attractive, medieval county town of **Warwick**, not far from Birmingham but in terms of bleakness a world away. There, Edith, a devout and practicing member of the Church of England, began her tutorship into the Roman Catholic Church in order that she and Ronald could be married. However, with Ronald fully immersed in the hectic social, political, and **academic life of Oxford**, Edith began to feel frustrated with her lot. She was isolated not just from Ronald, who visited Warwick infrequently, but also from her Cheltenham friends and Church of England community. Tolkien on the other hand was becoming an important figure in the culture of Exeter College; he was now **president of the debating society** and had a new interest in the societal intrigues of Oxford life.

William Morris

During his studies, Tolkien had little interest in any **post-Chaucerian English**, and, as a linguist, the college expected little of him in terms of the study of modern literature. Therefore, he was surprised to find a deep resonance with the fantastical works of **William Morris**, a former Exeter student. Morris' novel, *The House of the Wolfings* in particular, impressed Tolkien for its use of poetry and strange archaic language to instill an atmosphere of the ancient within the prose. Soon after, late in the summer of 1914, Tolkien wrote a long poem entitled "The Voyage of Earendel the Evening Star." Inspired by the works he had studied, it was a completely original work that marked the beginning of **Tolkien's own mythology**.

3-Second Quest
With the move from Classics to English, Tolkien completely immersed himself in the medieval texts he was so passionate about, and spent more time on his own languages and mythologies.

Related Thoughts
see also
OXFORD FOR GOOD
page 38
TEACHER AND SCHOLAR
page 40

[On reading the Cynewulf lines about the star Earendel]
❝ *There was something very remote and strange and beautiful behind those words, if I could grasp it, far beyond ancient English.* **❞**

J.R.R. TOLKIEN: A BIOGRAPHY

A TALE OF THE HOUSE OF THE WOLFINGS AND ALL THE KINDREDS OF THE MARK WRITTEN IN PROSE AND IN VERSE BY WILLIAM MORRIS.

WHILES IN THE EARLY WINTER EVE
WE PASS AMID THE GATHERING NIGHT
SOME HOMESTEAD THAT WE HAD TO LEAVE
YEARS PAST ; AND SEE ITS CANDLES BRIGHT
SHINE IN THE ROOM BESIDE THE DOOR
WHERE WE WERE MERRY YEARS AGONE
BUT NOW MUST NEVER ENTER MORE,
AS STILL THE DARK ROAD DRIVES US ON.
E'EN SO THE WORLD OF MEN MAY TURN
AT EVEN OF SOME HURRIED DAY
AND SEE THE ANCIENT GLIMMER BURN
ACROSS THE WASTE THAT HATH NO WAY;
THEN WITH THAT FAINT LIGHT IN ITS EYES
A WHILE I BID IT LINGER NEAR
AND NURSE IN WAVERING MEMORIES
THE BITTER-SWEET OF DAYS THAT WERE.

LONDON 1889: REEVES AND TURNER 196

William Morris

The House of the Wolfings
by William Morris

The *Poetic Edda*

The Great War

Published poet

As Britain declared war on Germany in 1914, Tolkien joined a program that allowed him to prepare for war while finishing his studies. He managed to complete his English degree as well as develop further his **invented languages**. He also attempted his first short story in verse and prose. Heavily influenced by William Morris' style, it was a dramatic retelling of "The Story of Kullervo" from the *Kalevala*. Afterwards, still meeting with the T.C.B.S after all these years, Tolkien declared he was to **become a poet**. Although unremarkable and quite detached from the trends of modern poetics, Tolkien's work showed a distinct style and with "Goblin Feet," a poem he soon detested for its kitsch representation of faery, Tolkien had his first **published work.**

Western Front

With embarkation to France imminent, Ronald and Edith, aware of the astonishingly grim mortality rate of the British soldiers there, married on March 22, 1916. Very soon after, **Signal Officer Tolkien** traveled to Calais. While billeted, he wrote many letters to Edith and some poems. He even managed to meet up with the other three members of the original **T.C.B.S.**—Christopher Wiseman, Robert Gilson, and Geoffrey Bache Smith (Ronald's oldest and dearest friends). Each man was an officer in a different battalion, and when they were transported to the **Western Front** for the Big Push on June 30, 1916, it was Tolkien who would be the last of the four to see action amid the hell and mud of the trenches.

The Somme

In one of the most bloody battles in the history of warfare, J. R. R. Tolkien saw his first and only action of the First World War. As thousands of slowly advancing British and French soldiers were cut down by German machine-gun fire in the **fields of the Somme**, Tolkien returned to his trench time after time physically unharmed. The landscape was pummeled into a featureless, muddy netherworld. Tolkien and his T.C.B.S. friends talked about poetry and war and how the world could possibly go on after such manmade horrors. By the time Tolkien was taken down with "trench fever" and returned to hospital in England, both Robert Gilson and Geoffrey Bache Smith had been killed. The bond of the **fellowship was forever broken**.

3-Second Quest

His experiences in the trenches in the First World War were to have a profound effect on Tolkien. The devastated landscapes, apocalyptic carnage, and personal loss cast an enduring shadow over his life and work.

Related Thoughts
see also
WARTIME IN OXFORD
page 52
THE WRITER'S CONCERNS
page 100

❝ My 'Sam Gamgee' is indeed a reflection of the English soldier, of the privates and batmen I knew in the 1914 war, and recognized as so far superior to myself. **❞**

J.R.R. TOLKIEN: A BIOGRAPHY

**Tolkien's pistol from
the First World War**

**French soldiers,
First World War**

Tolkien

...ley .455 Mark VI revolver carried by Second Lieutenant John
...n during his service with the 11th Battalion. The Lancashire
...ers on the Somme. Tolkien served as Battalion Signalling Officer
...m July 1916 onwards his battalion went in and out of the line
...he northern sector of the Somme. At the end of October
...contracted trench fever and was sent back to hospital in
...gham. He remained unfit for the rest of the war.

A New Mythology

A grand mythology

On his return from the battlefields of France, imbued with a sense of purpose and debt to his fallen brothers from the T.C.B.S. with whom he had shared so much **creative ambition**, Tolkien began to devise his epic. With Edith by his side, and in the English countryside that he so adored, he made notes and sketches of stories with the aim of creating a **grand mythology** stretching from the realm of the gods to that of earthly romances, from the dawn of time to the end of time. From far away, Christopher Wiseman wrote and encouraged him that now was the time to begin his masterwork. What Tolkien began was to become a work that would occupy much of his life—***The Silmarillion***.

A contented family

As severe recurrent illnesses prevented Tolkien from returning to the Western Front for the remainder of the war, he was able to work intensely on what he believed to be his life's work. On November 16, 1917, Edith gave birth to their first child, **John Francis Reuel**. This was a contented time for the Tolkiens, with Edith copying Ronald's stories into a large exercise book and the new family taking long walks around the woodlands that surrounded their **Staffordshire home**. As the war began to draw to an end, he attained a lucrative position as Assistant Lexicographer at the **New English Dictionary**, and the family moved to Oxford. Tolkien's love of words was put to good use, and the dictionary entries that he worked on included the words "waistcoat," "walnut," **"walrus,"** and "wampum."

The young professor

On a whim almost, Tolkien applied for a job at the **University of Leeds**. To his and Edith's surprise, he was offered the position; and they moved up to the north of England in October 1920. The new job coincided with the birth of their second son, **Michael Hilary Reuel**. At first, Tolkien deeply regretted moving his young family to the tough industrial city of Leeds after the dreaming spires of Oxford, but soon he and Edith found friends. In 1924, at the remarkably young age of 32, Tolkien was made a **Professor of English Language**. He went on to become a major contributor to what was to evolve into the best English department in the country.

3-Second Quest
Tolkien found fruitful employ on the New English Dictionary and then at the University of Leeds, while all the time planning the mythology that would underpin his lifetime's work.

Related Thoughts
see also
OXFORD FOR GOOD
page 38
THE SILMARILLION
page 96

[On his students at Leeds]
❝ *I am wholly in favour of 'dull stodges.' A surprisingly large proportion prove 'educable:' for which a primary qualification is the willingness to do work.* **❞**

J.R.R. TOLKIEN: A BIOGRAPHY

Oxford for Good

A return to the dreaming spires

In 1925 Tolkien was offered the Professorship of Anglo-Saxon at **Pembroke College, Oxford**, where he was to remain in post for the next 20 years. After the birth of their third son, Christopher Reuel, in 1924, Edith was extremely pleased to give birth to a daughter, Priscilla, in 1929. Life in Oxford was incredibly rewarding for the Tolkiens. Ronald was a **favorite lecturer** among undergraduates, who fed off his passion, sense of humor, and personable style of lecturing (despite his famously odd speech patterns). He formed, with a group of other dons, a late-night reading group dedicated to the discussion of the **Icelandic sagas**, all the while continuing to write and revise the tales of *The Silmarillion*.

Out of the ordinary

The man who created the fantastic worlds of *The Silmarillion*, *The Hobbit*, and *The Lord of the Rings* appeared quite ordinary. Indeed, it could be said that Tolkien was the **epitome of ordinariness**, his academic brilliance aside. The Tolkien family lived on **Northmoor Road in the suburbs of Oxford** and got by on the modest income that his professorship provided. There were no fancy clothes or expensive holidays, but there was time to explore neighboring villages and take short country walks. Tolkien became well known later in life as a private man, content socializing with his close circle of Oxford friends and his family, but in this isolated world he was developing **kingdoms in his imagination**.

A man who cared

For someone who was, to look at him, so ordinary, what marked Tolkien out as a lecturer and a public figure around Oxford was his **passionate** and humane character. Nobody could claim that Tolkien was a cold and distant presence like some of his faculty colleagues. He grew extremely hurt and impassioned at the thought of the encroachment of the ugly industrial world on his beloved English countryside; visits to the **much-changed landmarks** of his childhood, such as Sarehole, left him particularly upset. Tolkien was, in essence, a kind man and a great lover of people, most comfortable in the company of friends. All his life he made friends easily, unfazed by any suggested **class divide** that his position at Oxford implied.

3-Second Quest
As the family settled in Oxford, Tolkien proved an exceptionally popular lecturer and colleague, leading a vibrant professional and social existence at the university.

Related Thoughts
see also
OXFORD
page 30
FAMILY LIFE
page 44

❝ *I have a very simple sense of humor, which even my appreciative critics find tiresome.* **❞**
J.R.R. TOLKIEN: A BIOGRAPHY

Oxford High Street

10135 - OXFORD, HIGH STREET.

The Tolkien house,
Northmoor Road,
Oxford

Teacher and Scholar

The *Beowulf* lectures

Tolkien was an extremely popular teacher at Leeds and then Oxford, although his most comfortable environment was not always the lecture hall. Since childhood, Ronald had been an **uneasy speaker**, having a tripping, quick delivery that seemed to skip toward its audience. At times, he found it tricky to keep his lectures succinct, often finding that his vast breadth of subject knowledge forced him off on to irresistible tangents. But what most of his students remember fondly is his **contagious passion** for his subject, his immense intellectual prowess, and, most famously, the dramatic presentation of his lectures on *Beowulf*.

The bard

One of his students recalled years later how Tolkien would transform the classroom into a **mead hall** in which he was the bard and the students were the feasting, listening guests. Along with his colleagues, who included a certain C. S. Lewis, Tolkien was a part of an extremely popular and dynamic department of what was hitherto believed a dry-as-dust academic area. The poet **W. H. Auden**, who was an undergraduate at Oxford during this time, wrote many years later to Tolkien to thank him for his lectures all those years before. Auden wrote that it was an unforgettable experience to watch Tolkien recite the **Old English of the original *Beowulf*** poem to a full lecture in a voice that, he mused, was the voice of Gandalf.

The perfectionist

Even by the scrupulous standards of the field of philology, Tolkien's attention to detail, to the patterns and historical **spirals of words**, marked a truly special dedication to his work that was nothing less than obsessive. He was very much a linguistic detective, often finding overarching truths from **painstaking research** into seemingly unconnected philological facts. He lectured an extraordinary number of hours during term time, as well as serving as an external examiner for a wide array of British universities, always aware of the family he needed to support. On top of this, he redesigned the nature of the English syllabus at Oxford and published some of the most significant philological essays of the 1930s, including his groundbreaking lecture "***Beowulf: The Monsters and the Critics***" in 1934.

3-Second Quest
Tolkien was a popular lecturer at both Leeds and Oxford, his subject area seeing a dramatic increase in student numbers during these years.

Related Thoughts
see also
SCHOOL YEARS
page 24
STUDYING MYTHS
page 32

"A dragon is no idle fancy. Even today you may find men not ignorant of tragic legend and history, who have heard of heroes and indeed seen them, who have yet been caught by the fascination of the worm."
BEOWULF: THE MONSTERS AND THE CRITICS, 1934

Poet W. H. Auden

Beowulf manuscript from between the 8th and 11th centuries

1904 German edition of *Beowulf*

The Inklings

A strong bond

One of the most famous friendships in all of English literature is that between J. R. R. Tolkien and the author of *The Chronicles of Narnia*, **Clive Staples Lewis**. As colleagues, Tolkien on the language side and Lewis on the literature side, they worked tirelessly to bring the two factions of the English faculty together for the betterment of the university. As friends, they provided a constant source of support, criticism, and **intellectual stimulation** for one another. They became so close that when Lewis wrote about the platonic bond that can occur between two men in his book *The Four Loves*, it was of Tolkien he wrote. They connected through their war experiences, their passion for **Norse sagas**, and, as Lewis was in the process of converting to Christianity at the time they met, their faith in God.

The Eagle and Child

In 1931 Tolkien and Lewis began attending a reading group called **The Inklings** in which the members read aloud and criticized each other's unpublished creative work. When this original group disbanded, the name was adopted by the two as the moniker for their band of friends, all male, all Christian, and most interested in literature, who would meet regularly around Lewis in **The Eagle and Child pub** in Oxford. Rather than an intense and ambitious collective, it was a casual gathering of sincere friends and literary minds. On a Thursday evening they would gather at Lewis's rooms at **Magdalen College**, light a large fire, and take it in turns to read their stories. The Inklings are now part of literary history.

A nurturing atmosphere

The Inklings were a formidable bunch. Although the "**membership**" was a fluid one, the main attendees were "Warnie" Lewis (C. S. Lewis's brother), R. E. Harvard (an Oxford doctor), Owen Barfield (a solicitor), and Hugo Dyson, the Professor of English at Reading University. Added to this, when war came in 1939, was the extremely charismatic novelist and poet Charles Williams, who worked for the **Oxford University Press**. The group would drink and smoke their pipes and read aloud the latest chapters of their works-in-progress, each giving advice and encouragement to the other, even suggesting cuts and additions. It was among this company of genial and **enthusiastic lovers of literature** that Tolkien began circulating his work, starting with his much toiled over chapters of *The Silmarillion*.

3-Second Quest
It is quite conceivable that without the nurturing atmosphere and sounding board of The Inklings, Tolkien would never have completed the works that made his name.

Related Thoughts
see also
THE GREAT WAR
page 34
OXFORD FOR GOOD
page 38

❝ *Every writer making a secondary world wishes in some measure to be a real maker, or hopes that he is drawing on reality.* **❞**
ON FAIRY STORIES

The Eagle and Child,
Oxford

C. S. LEWIS,
his brother, W. H. Lewis, J. R. R. Tolkien,
Charles Williams and other friends
met every Tuesday morning, between
the years 1939-1962 in the back room
of this their favourite pub. These men,
popularly known as the "Inklings", met
here to drink Beer and to discuss,
among other things, the books they
were writing.

C. S. Lewis

Magdalen College, Oxford

Oxford Life

The scholar's wife

Edith Tolkien was deeply devoted to her husband, but found the role of **scholar's wife in Oxford** more than a little difficult to adjust to. During their first stint in Oxford she had made few friends, being naturally shy and uninterested in academic pursuits. In Leeds, a much less rigid scholastic environment, she made many friends among the faculty and even some lifelong friends among Ronald's pupils, who often came to the house for tutorials. But **back in Oxford** she found herself isolated once again with her husband's new devotion to his male friends in The Inklings. Despite this, the deeply held affection that Ronald and Edith had for each other was never in doubt, and she often provided him with a muse, most famously as the inspiration for the Elves **Lúthien Tinúviel** and **Arwen Evenstar**.

Working together

Despite Edith's challenges with life in Oxford, she was a much-cherished friend to those she made, and she and Ronald were **devoted to their family**. The children were doted on, and both Ronald and Edith would beam with pride at every small achievement. Tolkien was a particularly warm and loving father, never averse to public displays of affection or even **eccentric entertainments** such as his sense of humor would conjure. After the purchase of their **first car**, the Tolkiens would go on trips to the seaside—although Ronald was often dangerously adventurous behind the wheel—and visit family friends such as the now aged Father Francis and Ronald's brother Hilary, who had a fruit farm near Evesham.

The children

The four Tolkien children remember an extremely **happy childhood**, and all went on to make their parents immensely proud. John, the eldest son, became a Catholic priest. Michael was awarded the **George Medal** for his heroic services during the Battle of Britain. After the war, he finished his degree and taught Classics at Stoneyhurst College, a prestigious Catholic private school in Lancashire. Christopher, who went on to become a **Fellow at New College**, Oxford, lecturing in Middle English, Anglo-Saxon, and Old Norse, was a close collaborator with his father as he wrote his famous books. He even became a member of The Inklings. Priscilla, the Tolkiens' long-awaited daughter, became a public face of her father's legacy and became a patron of many **charities and conventions**.

3-Second Quest
Tolkien was a dedicated family man and loving father whose enthusiasm for amusing and entertaining his children became the foundations of his books.

Related Thoughts
see also
OXFORD FOR GOOD
page 38
AFTER TOLKIEN
page 104

❝ *She was (and knew she was) my Lúthien. I will say no more now.* **❞**

The undersigned, having just partaken of your ham, have drunk your health:

C. S. Lewis. Fellow of Magdalen, sometime scholar of University College Tol 13th Light Infantry

H. V. D. Dyson Fellow of Merton College, Lecturer of University College, University Lecturer in English Literature. Formerly sometime lecturer of Reading College, Queen's Own Royal West Kent Regt 1915-19.

David Cecil Fellow of New College — ex-Fellow of Wadham College — University Lecturer in English Literature. Commoner of Christ Church.

W. H. Lewis. Royal Military College, Sandhurst, Regular Army 1914-1932, World War II 1939-45. Major. Retired pay.

Colin Hardie Fellow and Tutor in Classics of Magdalen College University Lecturer in Greek and Latin Literature, formerly Director of the British School at Rome, and Fellow, Scholar & Exhibitioner of Balliol College Secretary of the Oxford Dante Society (founded 1878) Sector Warden ARP service Oxford.

Christopher Reuel Tolkien. B.A. Undergraduate of Trinity College. Late R.A.F.

R Emlyn Havard M.A. D.M. Oxon. B.A. Cantab. late Schorstein Research Fellow University of Oxford late Lecturer in Physiology Guys Hospital Demonstrator in Biochemistry University of Oxford, late Surgeon R.N.V.R.

John Ronald Reuel Tolkien M.A. Merton Professor of English Language & Literature, late professor of Anglo-Saxon (Pembroke College), and exhibitioner of Exeter College and of the Lancashire Fusiliers (1914-8) and father of the above-named C.R.T.

The Inklings members, listed in the Eagle and Child

The front door of the _____ Tolkien house

The Stories

From the North Pole

Ever since Ronald and Edith's eldest son, John, was a small child, Tolkien had enjoyed creating **adventure stories** with simple but dynamic characters for the entertainment of his children. For year after year every Christmas, the household received a long, illustrated letter from **Father Christmas** detailing a year in the life of the North Pole. By this point, Tolkien was an exceptionally accomplished artist, and the colorful and detailed artwork that accompanied the letters (and soon the stories he would commit to paper) were a significant factor in the enchantment. By the time the family had moved to Leeds, Tolkien was creating elaborate and good-humored **bedtime tales** for his young boys.

The prose writer

As well as Tolkien's progress in his academic works during the 20's and 30's, the stories he was creating for his family's amusement were setting him on a pathway that would lead to both *The Hobbit* and *The Lord of the Rings*. It was during this time that Tolkien began not only to simplify his **storytelling technique** but also take the possibilities of prose seriously. Although he was still **composing poetry**, he was now committing to paper works that would become *Mr. Bliss*, *Roverandom*, and *Farmer Giles of Ham*. This was in part due to a conversation he had with C. S. Lewis in which they decided, on seeing so few stories published that they wanted to read, to write "**great romances**" themselves.

The blank page

In the summer of 1928 Tolkien was marking **School Certificate exam papers**—a duty he took on every summer in order to supplement his income. As the story goes, trudging through paper after paper in his study by an open window, he came upon a blank page "which is the best thing that can happen to an examiner," he recalled many years later. As Tolkien himself told it, on that blank page he began to write: "**In a hole in the ground there lived a hobbit.**" At this point Tolkien had no idea what a hobbit was (he had recently read and admired Sinclair Lewis's novel *Babbitt*), and on reflecting upon the sentence he thought he had better find out what hobbits were and what they were like.

3-Second Quest
Now settled in Oxford, Tolkien was creating imaginative tales that derived from his wish to entertain his children, and he began committing them to paper.

Related Thoughts
see also
THE HOBBIT
page 48
WRITING **THE HOBBIT**
page 66

❝ *I find it only too easy to write opening chapters, and at the moment the story is not unfolding.* **❞**

The HOBBIT

or There and Back Again

by J. R. R. TOLKIEN

Illustrated by the author

HOUGHTON MIFFLIN COMPANY BOSTON

The Hobbit title page

Writing *The Hobbit*

The unfinished adventure

For quite some time (years, in fact), the entire existence of the race of hobbits remained just **one sentence on the blank page** of an exam paper. The only other development Tolkien carried out was to construct Thror's map, the ancient document that would eventually lead **Bilbo Baggins** on his quest. Even as Tolkien returned to the idea, like so many other tales he devised at this time, the story remained unfinished and largely uncommitted to paper. For many years he would tell the story of the Baggins adventure to his young children at bedtime, and he created a variety of **indulgent tangents and impromptu endings** that would never make it into print.

The publishing venture

One of the few to have seen the typed (and unfinished) manuscript of *The Hobbit* was one of Tolkien's former students and now family friend, **Elaine Griffiths**. When Elaine began some editorial work for the London publishers George Allen & Unwin, she recommended that they approach Professor Tolkien and ask to see his **wonderful children's story**. Tolkien happily showed them the manuscript, and they looked upon it enthusiastically, asking him to finish the story for consideration for publication the following year. Tolkien set to work, and, in **October 1936**, the publishers received the completed manuscript. Chairman Stanley Unwin gave the book to his 10-year-old son, **Rayner**, to read, and he responded with a positive one-page report. It was this response that convinced Unwin to publish the book.

The bestseller

The Hobbit was published by **George Allen & Unwin** on September 21, 1937. Although Tolkien was concerned as to the reaction of his Oxford colleagues, who may have wondered how Tolkien had been spending the time and money afforded him by various research grants, the publication went largely unnoticed in academe. In the literary world, however, *The Hobbit* received **favorable reviews** (not least from C. S. Lewis in *The Times* and its *Literary Supplement*). The book was also received very well in the US, and it won the *New York Herald Tribune* prize for the best **children's book of the year**. By the end of 1937, Tolkien's publishers were beginning to realize they had a best-selling children's author on their hands.

3-Second Quest
With the publication of *The Hobbit*, Tolkien soon became a recognized children's author of dynamic adventures. Little did the world know the true depths of his imagination.

Related Thoughts
see also
THE TRILOGY
page 54
THE HOBBIT
page 66

❝ Middle-earth is our world. I have (of course) placed the action in a purely imaginary period of antiquity, in which the shape of the continental masses was different. **❞**

Elaine Griffiths.

with best
wishes
from
J.R.R.T

The
Hobbit
by
J. R. R.
Tolkien

The
Hobbit

George Allen
/Unwin Ltd

Rayner Unwin

The Children's Author

The real hobbit

Tolkien, much later in life, reflected on the origins of hobbits. He commented often on how they represented his experience of the people native to the **English countryside** and represented, in many ways, a traditional English "type." But he was also able to draw parallels between his popular creation and himself. After all, he had a special connection to the lush **green rolling lands** of the English countryside that dated back to his childhood and the happy times at Sarehole with his mother. He also enjoyed ale, was an avid **pipe-smoker**, was unadventurous in his travels and tastes, and liked the simple things in life. He even noted how, as the years went on, he liked to wear colorful waistcoats.

The next book

Stanley Unwin, Tolkien's publisher, keen to **build upon the success** of *The Hobbit*, held many meetings with its author in the months following publication to work out what to publish next. Tolkien offered most of his almost-ready manuscripts, including *Mr. Bliss*, *Farmer Giles of Ham*, and even, eventually, *The Silmarillion*. Unwin, who liked them all—especially parts of *The Silmarillion*—felt none of them was quite right for the next book. It was becoming obvious that what the **public wanted was more hobbits**. Realizing this also, Tolkien—who had initially thought he had explored all there was to explore in the character of **Bilbo Baggins**—began to contemplate what could constitute further adventures for the inhabitants of the Shire.

A darker adventure

Tolkien decided to write the adventures of Bilbo's nephew, Bingo Baggins. He identified one of the **underexplored elements** of *The Hobbit* as the origins of the magical ring that Bilbo had found in the lair of the creature **Gollum**. Through the fall of 1939, as he wrote in his study late into the night on the backs of old exam papers, the story became larger, wider, and much darker than the "children's story" of *The Hobbit*. It was something, in fact, closer in feel to *The Silmarillion*, which was never intended for children. Tolkien began to realize the seriousness of the tone and themes of his new work, and, unhappy with the name of his protagonist, **renamed him Frodo**.

3-Second Quest

Much time was spent pinning down the follow-up to *The Hobbit*—a work that was never supposed to have a sequel. After the rejection of *The Silmarillion*, Tolkien decided to write more about the halfling heroes.

Related Thoughts

see also
THE HOBBIT
page 66
SHORTER WORKS
page 98

❝ *Fantasy is escapist, and that is its glory. If a soldier is imprisoned by the enemy, don't we consider it his duty to escape?* **❞**

Wartime in Oxford

Comfort in routine

In the aftermath of the publication of *The Hobbit*, and as the new story was being developed and written—expanding and deepening as it went—Tolkien continued to work within the comfortable **regimentation of academic life**. He delivered famous lectures around the country, most notably his groundbreaking lecture on *Beowulf* and the annual **Andrew Lang Lecture** on fairy stories at the **University of St. Andrews**, Scotland. In 1939, as Britain went to war with Nazi Germany, Tolkien found that the greatest disruption to his life was in the minutiae of the domestic routine. The three boys had all left home, domestic help became difficult to find, and **evacuees** and lodgers were sometimes accommodated.

A huge enterprise

Tolkien was one of the few Oxford dons who was not commissioned to contribute work to the **War Office** during the war. As the war progressed, the professor witnessed the university change to suit students preparing to fight for their country. Against the **background of drastic events** in the world, Tolkien pressed on with his writing. He was aware by this point that he was **creating an epic so expansive** that at times he felt it was getting out of hand. It appears there were moments when it all became too much, and there were several periods of no writing at all, including the whole of 1940.

Close friends no more

In 1945, as the war ended and Oxford attempted to return to a state of normality, Tolkien was appointed **Merton Professor of English Language and Literature**. One of his responsibilities was to sit on the board of electors for the vacated position of Professor of English Literature at the same college. Tolkien's **lukewarm support** for his old friend C. S. Lewis (who was passed over for the position) seemed to mark the beginning of a **"cooling-off" period** for their friendship over the next few decades. Although Tolkien continued to seek Lewis' responses to his work, he more often than not ignored the advice, and the two friends gradually saw less and less of each other. Also, Tolkien found it deeply difficult to hide his dislike for Lewis's *Narnia* stories, which began with a reading to The Inklings of *The Lion, the Witch and the Wardrobe* in 1949.

3-Second Quest
Although the war had little effect on Tolkien's work at Oxford, it did afford him the time and space to concentrate on the sequel to *The Hobbit*; time that he did not always use.

Related Thoughts
see also
THE GREAT WAR
page 34
OXFORD FOR GOOD
page 38

❝ I have in this war a burning private grudge against that ruddy little ignoramus Adolf Hitler for... making forever accursed, that noble northern spirit, a supreme contribution to Europe. **❞**

Merton College, Oxford

Oxford in wartime

Evacuees awaiting a train to the countryside

The Trilogy

The return of Rayner

In the summer of 1947 **Rayner Unwin**, Stanley's son who had given his book report as a young boy on *The Hobbit*, was shown a "finished" typescript of *The Lord of the Rings*. Now an undergraduate at Oxford, and a friend of Tolkien's, he recommended heartily that his father's firm should **publish the book**. Stanley passed on Rayner's report to Tolkien who took exception to two comments that would persist throughout the public life of *The Lord of the Rings*. They were the comparison to Wagner's ***Nibelungenlied*** and the assertion that the story was an allegory. Tolkien hated both suggestions until his dying day, retaining a particular dislike for literary allegory of all kinds.

Interwoven stories

In the autumn of 1949, after many months of "niggling" over every sentence of the huge manuscript, Tolkien painstakingly typed up his book and posted a copy to C. S. Lewis. Lewis's response beamed with enthusiasm for the "**substantial splendor**" of the work. He wrote, "[it is] almost unequaled in the whole range of narrative art known to me." A book **12 years in the making** was now complete, but the journey to print would be a long and difficult one. One problem lay in Tolkien's belief that *The Lord of the Rings* and *The Silmarillion* were completely **interdependent texts** and that the new book, yet to be seen by Stanley Unwin, could not possibly be published without the older one, which Unwin had already rejected many years before.

Three stories, but one book

After much wrangling, and even flirtation with another publisher, Tolkien agreed to relent on his intentions for *The Silmarillion*. Eventually, it fell to Rayner Unwin, now working at his father's firm, to oversee the publication of *The Lord of the Rings*. Due to the **unusual nature of the book**, the high cost of paper in postwar Britain, and the sheer size of the manuscript, Tolkien reluctantly agreed to have the book released in **three volumes**. He gave subtitles to each one, despite the book being one continuous narrative rather than a trilogy. On July 29, 1954 (16 years after the publication of *The Hobbit*), the world was presented with ***The Fellowship of the Ring***.

3-Second Quest
The journey to publication for *The Lord of the Rings* was a fittingly long and difficult adventure, but the book was eventually delivered with love and care by George Allen & Unwin in 1954.

Related Thoughts
see also
WRITING *THE HOBBIT*
page 48
THE 'SEQUEL'
page 74

❝ *The Lord of the Rings is written in my life blood, such as that is, thick or thin; and I can no other.* **❞**

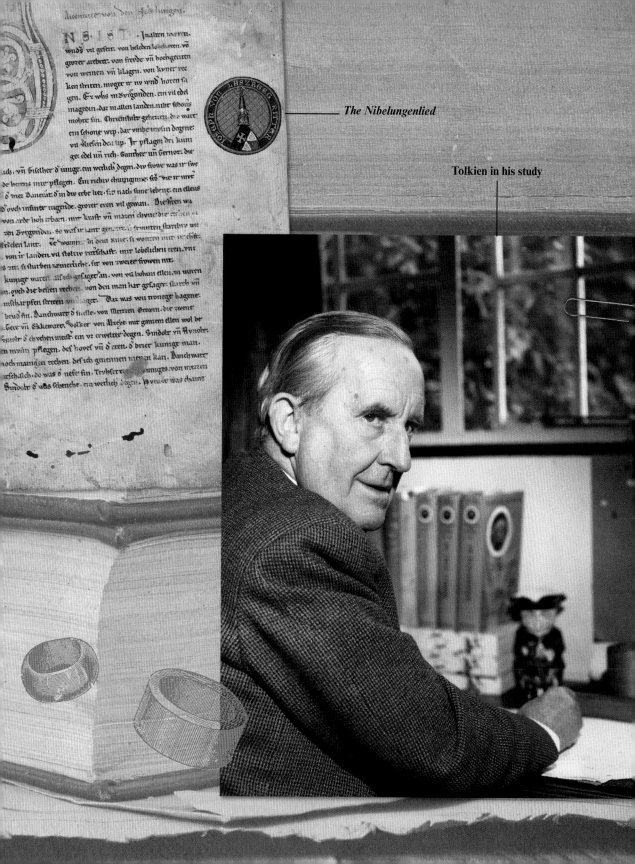

The Nibelungenlied

Tolkien in his study

Success

Readers' reponses

By October 1955 all three volumes of *The Lord of the Rings* had been published, and critics and fans alike could judge the book in its entirety. It soon became clear (and this remained the case for the rest of Tolkien's life) that the book **polarized the reading public**. Those who championed it, such as C. S. Lewis and W. H. Auden, sang its praises in the most exalting language, calling it a **masterpiece of all literature**. Those who did not take to it found it childish, boyish, and without truly rounded characters. But the popularity of *The Lord of the Rings* grew and Tolkien now found much of his time outside of academic duties taken up with replying to **fan mail**.

Published without permission

The books sold well and steadily for many years in hardback, but it wasn't until a publisher in New York City, **Ace Books**, printed an unauthorized paperback copy in 1965 that sales really began to take off. Consequent actions by Tolkien, his publishers, and, most remarkably, his growing army of fans in the US, meant that not only were Ace Books eventually forced to pay Tolkien royalties for every book they had sold, but an authorized paperback took its place on **best seller lists**. Soon *The Lord of the Rings* had outsold *The Lord of the Flies* and *The Catcher in the Rye*. American students especially took to **Frodo's adventures**, establishing fan clubs and forcing the book to be taken seriously by US academe.

In demand

Although Tolkien was a creature of routine, his natural politeness meant that for some time he found it very difficult not to grant an audience to **many fans** who called on him in Oxford. In the 1960s, these visitors began to include Americans who made **pilgrimages to see the great man**, members of The Tolkien Society of America, and top academics keen to discuss Tolkien's worlds and the now much-anticipated volume—*The Silmarillion*. Tolkien grew very quickly to **dislike the attention**, particularly that afforded him by the press. Despite being a lover of company, on his retirement from Oxford in 1959, Tolkien began to spend much of his time at home with Edith.

3-Second Quest
Although the book had done well for many years in hardback, the publicity surrounding the Ace Books debacle meant that by the end of 1968, *The Lord of the Rings* had sold in excess of three million copies worldwide.

Related Thoughts
see also
ENDURING POPULARITY
page 112
HIGH FANTASY
page 116

❝ *Being a cult figure in one's own lifetime I am afraid is not at all pleasant. However, I do not find that it tends to puff one up: in my case at any rate it makes me feel extremely small and inadequate.* **❞**

The Final Journey

Adjusting to retirement

After 40 years as an academic, living under the pressures and schedules of university life, Tolkien could be excused for finding **retirement in 1959** difficult to adjust to. Edith by this time was suffering from ill health, most affectingly an arthritic condition that hampered her mobility. This, along with the Tolkiens living some two miles (3 km) from the center of Oxford, meant that they began to see much less of their friends than they had done before. Invitations to college dinners and public events always came second to his **concerns for Edith's welfare** and so were rarely taken up. Tolkien wrote and published new works, although *The Silmarillion* **remained unfinished**.

By the sea

In 1968, in their late 70's, the Tolkiens decided to move to **Bournemouth**, a town with a large population that matched the Tolkiens very much in age and class. It was perhaps surprising that they chose to move so far from their beloved Oxford, but for years the Tolkiens had **enjoyed seaside holidays** there. Edith, who had never found it easy to make friends in her husband's Oxford circle, had many friends on the south coast as a result of these holidays. In Bournemouth, Edith was **extremely happy**, and Tolkien had the time and space (now that no fans could find him) to work on the massive task of creating a cohesive narrative for *The Silmarillion*.

Passing on the legacy

On November 29, 1971, after a short illness, Edith died, aged 82. With Edith gone, Tolkien saw no reason to remain in Bournemouth and returned to Oxford. Although suffering **deep grief**, Tolkien was happy to be back in the city of spires, dining at college and living the life of a wealthy man. He visited his children and his brother Hilary, and even spent some time with his oldest friend, **Christopher Wiseman**, from the T.C.B.S. days. Enmeshed once again in the technical webs of his own mythology, he confirmed that his **son Christopher** would complete *The Silmarillion* should Tolkien die before he was able. And on November 2, 1973, aged 81, after an abrupt illness, J. R. R. Tolkien, the man who created Middle-earth and all of its inhabitants, passed away.

3-Second Quest
Although the wide-open spaces of retirement were at times difficult for Tolkien, he wrote many works and was active in academic life right up to the end.

Related Thoughts
see also
OXFORD FOR GOOD
page 38
AFTER TOLKIEN
page 104

❝ *End? No, it doesn't end here. Death is just another path, one which we must all take. The grey rain-curtain of this world rolls back, and all change to silver glass... And then you see it... White shores, and beyond, a far green country, under a swift sunrise.* **❞**
GANDALF,
THE RETURN OF THE KING

The Tolkiens retreat to Bournemouth

Timeline

1892

John Ronald Reuel Tolkien is born to John and Mabel in Bloemfontein, South Africa. With the death of his father a few years later, the Tolkiens moved to Birmingham, England.

1900

The young Tolkien attends King Edward's School where he begins to study Latin and Old English. In 1904 his mother dies and he is taken into the care of Father Morgan at the Birmingham Oratory.

1908

Tolkien falls in love with fellow orphan Edith Bratt, but they are forbidden to be together until Tolkien has turned 21. In the meantime, he gains entry to Oxford University.

1916

After marrying Edith, Tolkien leaves for the trenches of France where he fights at the Somme. He returns home with trench fever. The following year the Tolkiens' first child, John, is born.

1918

Tolkien is appointed Assistant Lexicographer at the *New English Dictionary* in Oxford (the most enjoyable period of his professional life). He also undertakes tutorial work at the university.

1920

Tolkien takes a position in the English department at Leeds University where he is soon made Professor of English Language. His second son, Michael, is born.

1925

A year after the birth of his third son, Christopher, Ronald moves the family back to Oxford where he is appointed the Rawlinson and Bosworth Professor of Anglo-Saxon at Pembroke College.

1931

A couple of years after the birth of the Tolkiens' daughter, Priscilla, Ronald is very much a fixture in Oxonian academic life, and he becomes a founding member of The Inklings with friend C. S. Lewis.

1933

Tolkien begins to populate his children's bedtime stories with strange little creatures called hobbits. The subsequent story he writes down over the next few years forms the basis for his greatest epic.

1939–45

During the Second World War, life in Oxford is barely disturbed, but Tolkien's sequel to *The Hobbit* suffers long periods of inattention.

1959

Tolkien retires as Professor of English Language at Oxford and dedicates himself to Edith, who begins to suffer increasingly from ill health.

1965

With the paperback publication of *The Lord of the Rings*, Tolkien's fame reaches a wholly unexpected level on a global scale. Although diligent, he does not fully enjoy the new attention afforded him by media and fans.

1968

Ronald and Edith move to Bournemouth on the south coast of England to escape public intrusion and live a peaceful life.

1971

Edith dies in Bournemouth after a short but severe illness. Tolkien, with nothing to keep him on the coast, returns to Oxford to live near his beloved university.

1973

J. R. R. Tolkien dies at the age of 81 while visiting friends in Bournemouth.

Glossary

Apolausticks A club founded by Tolkien at Exeter College to discuss papers with fellow intellectuals.

Beowulf An Anglo-Saxon poem, in which the hero Beowulf encounters three monsters, including a dragon. Tolkien lectured with great success about the work.

Birmingham Oratory After his mother died, Tolkien spent much time at the Roman Catholic community where his guardian Father Francis lived and worked.

Edith Bratt Tolkien's wife, whom he fell in love with as a teenager in a boarding house in Birmingham. They were married in 1916. Edith died in 1971.

Comparative philology The study of linguistics that compares language systems to discover if they have a common ancestor.

Crist At university, Tolkien read this poem attributed to Cynewulf and came across *Midden-erde*, Middle English for "Middle-earth."

Exeter College The Oxford University college where Tolkien lived and studied. He read Classics before transferring to Comparative philology.

C. S. Lewis A close friend and colleague of Tolkien's, a member of The Inklings, and the author of *The Chronicles of Narnia*.

Inklings, The An Oxford group, including Tolkien and C. S. Lewis, that met to read aloud and discuss their works.

Kalevala A narrative poem combining Finnish folk tales with a world of myths that were the inspiration for his first short story in verse and prose.

King Edward's School The secondary school that Tolkien attended. Teacher George Brewerton encouraged him to read Anglo-Saxon works and Arthurian legends.

Andrew Lang A collector of fairy stories and myths. Tolkien read his works as a boy.

George MacDonald A 19th-century fantasy novelist of works such as *The Princess and the Goblin*. He was an early influence for Tolkien.

Father Francis Xavier Morgan Tolkien's guardian after his mother died, Father Francis looked after Tolkien's wellbeing in Birmingham.

Sarehole A hamlet in Birmingham where Tolkien lived after his father's death. Its idyllic landscape was the inspiration for the hobbits' Shire in Tolkien's novels.

Sir Gawain and the Green Knight A Middle English Arthurian romance that Tolkien read at school.

T. C. B. S. (Tea Club Barrovian Society) Tolkien's group of friends from King Edward's who met to share their written work. Two of the T. C. B. S. were killed in the First World War.

The House of the Wolfings The William Morris novel in which the use of archaic language and poetry inspired Tolkien to write the first work in his Middle-earth mythology.

Christopher Tolkien Tolkien's third son, born in 1924, collated the Middle-earth histories after his father's death.

Mabel Tolkien Tolkien's mother, who died from diabetes when Tolkien was 12 years old.

Chapter 2

Works

The Hobbit

A symbolic character

The race of the hobbits came from one sentence, idly jotted down one summer's afternoon on the blank page of an examination paper J. R. R. Tolkien was marking. But the **creation of the tales** and the peoples that inhabit them are all part of a much more complex story that stretches from Tolkien's own childhood and his academic studies. In many ways, **the hobbits** were the characters Tolkien was always destined to create, such was his love of the simple things in life, the **English countryside**, and his devotion to his friends. The hobbits came to symbolize everything that Tolkien held dear, and the links between his life and his works make for a fascinating study.

Improvised tales

The Tolkien children remember the story of *The Hobbit* as having many different aspects and more than one **improvised alternate ending**. Inspired by a favorite bedtime book for his children, *The Marvellous Land of the Snergs* by E. A. Wyke-Smith, in about 1926 J. R. R Tolkien began telling his **stories of hobbits**. Wyke-Smith's popular children's book tells of the adventures of two children, Sylvia and Joe, who are often assisted by a race of small, thick-set people who live in a secret kingdom on earth. Over many years, *The Hobbit* was developed slowly from different and unconnected impromptu oral tales made up by Tolkien to entertain his children. Informed by his **scholarly studies of dragon-slaying** and mythological quests, they became so much more than just bedtime stories, and were later absorbed into the tale of Bilbo Baggins as it was committed to paper.

The completed manuscript

The Hobbit was almost never finished in the form we have it. As his children grew older, it seems Tolkien saw less and less relevance in a completed, written version of *The Hobbit*. It required the interest of the publishers George Allen & Unwin to prompt him to revisit the typescript and set his mind to revising and finishing the story. **Returning to the tale**, Tolkien injected new weight to its themes, altered the fate of some main characters, and even changed some of the names. For instance, for much of the writing of *The Hobbit*, **Gandalf** was in fact the name of the head Dwarf, with the name Bladorthin given to the wizard. With new impetus, Tolkien had his story ready for publication in **December 1936**.

3-Second Quest
Tolkien's first published novel involving the inhabitants and mythologies of Middle-earth was, for much of its creation, a story for the entertainment of his children that was almost never finished.

Related Thoughts
see also
THE STORIES
page 46
WRITING *THE HOBBIT*
page 48

❝I should like to record my own love and my children's love of E. A. Wyke-Smith's Marvellous Land of Snergs, at any rate of the Snerg element of that tale.**❞**

THE ANNOTATED HOBBIT

An Unexpected Party

Dwarves on the doorstep

J. R. R. Tolkien's first published book introduced what has proved to be one of the most beloved creations in all of literature. **Hobbits**—little country folk about three-and-a-half feet (one meter) tall—would not only provide the central character (and atypical hero) for this first adventure in the **mapped world of Middle-earth** for the reading public but would go on to populate Tolkien's epic trilogy. The story of *The Hobbit* begins with the well-to-do hobbit Bilbo Baggins of Bag End, in the Shire, who has his comfortable, unadventurous life disrupted by a visit from the wizard Gandalf and 13 Dwarves, led by **Thorin Oakenshield**. We see from the start that Bilbo is a **reluctant hero**. His world before adventure is serene and comfortable—a far cry from the lands described beyond the Shire.

Smaug the Magnificent

Gandalf expressly informs Bilbo that he has come to recruit him for an adventure. Thorin explains, in a delightfully rustic and **chaotic opening** to the book, how his people were driven out of their homes, the underground halls beneath the **Lonely Mountain** that lies far to the east of the Shire, by the dragon Smaug the Magnificent. The Dwarves are on a mission to exact revenge upon the **ancient dragon** and reclaim the caves as their own. Gandalf, who has summoned the Dwarves to Bag End to meet Bilbo, the final member of their party, has a hard time convincing them that Bilbo is indeed the ideal candidate to be their "burglar."

Saved by the wizard

With reluctance on both sides, Bilbo joins the quest to reclaim the caves of the Lonely Mountain for the Dwarf lords and to steal the **hoard of treasure** on which Smaug sleeps. Shortly after setting out, the group is captured by three hungry trolls. Gandalf, **tricking the trolls** out into the sunlight where they turn to stone, releases the travelers from a grim fate. The group acquire an array of swords and other weaponry, some magical, from the plunder of the troll caves. Bilbo takes a sword for himself, which he later gives the name Sting. After this **narrow escape**, the band of adventurers find refuge in the valley of **Rivendell**, in the house of Elrond Halfelven, son of Eärendil.

3-Second Quest

Tolkien's beginning to *The Hobbit* is a rowdy introduction to both hobbits and Dwarves, setting the perfect tone for what many would come to see as a classic children's story.

Related Thoughts

see also
THE HOBBIT
page 66
BILBO AND THE WORLD
page 72

❝And yes, no doubt to others, our ways seem quaint, but, today of all days, it is brought home: it is no bad thing to celebrate the simple life.**❞**

BILBO BAGGINS,
THE FELLOWSHIP OF THE RING

ЭСГАРОТ

ЖЕЛЕЗНЫЕ ХОЛМЫ

ОДИНОКАЯ ГОРА

ДОЛГОЕ ОЗЕРО

ДЕЙЛ

Р. БЫСТРОТЕЧНАЯ

ДВОРЕЦ КОРОЛЯ ЭЛЬФОВ

ЧЁРНЫЙ ЛЕС

скала каррок

ДОМ БЕОРНА

ТУМАННЫЕ ГОРЫ

ПОСЛЕДНИЙ ДОМАШНИЙ ПРИЮТ

ДИКИЙ КРАЙ

ХОББИТОН

Ривенделл

С

З В

Ю

Slaying the Dragon

The creature Gollum

After the wise words of Elrond and his help with **Thror's map** (an ancient guide to Smaug's lair), the group travel on. When they are attacked by goblins beneath the Misty Mountains, **Gandalf leads the Dwarves** to safety, but they realize too late that they have lost Bilbo. As Bilbo tries to navigate his way in the labyrinthine cave system, he comes upon the creature Gollum, who lives by an **underground lake** on a diet of fish and goblin. On the cave floor, **Bilbo finds a ring**—a magic ring that Gollum does not realize he has lost. This ring has the power to make the wearer invisible, and Bilbo uses it to escape the caves and the grasp of the crazed creature.

A perilous route

Chased by goblins and evil wolves called Wargs, Bilbo, reunited with the group, makes it to the **forest of Mirkwood** with the help of a group of eagles and a were-bear named Beorn. Once in the dark forest, however, the group are without Gandalf (who has left them to deal with other urgent business), and dangers continue to imperil their journey. They are first **trapped by giant spiders** and then captured by a band of unfriendly Wood-elves. Bilbo employs the magic ring to help them all escape. Hiding in large wooden barrels, they **float down the river** that runs through the forest to Lake-town—a human settlement that exists in the shadow of the Lonely Mountain and the smoke of Smaug the Magnificent.

Bilbo's victory

Bilbo enters Smaug's lair via a **secret door**, and, although the dragon is angry at the intrusion, Bilbo talks with him. Smaug unwittingly reveals that he has a weak spot in his armorlike hide on his left breast. Furious that Bilbo has tricked him, the **dragon swoops on Lake-town** and sets fire to it. As he does so, the archer Bard—having been informed of Smaug's weak spot—kills him with one arrow. In the aftermath, Men, Dwarves, and Elves fight over Smaug's treasure, but the imminent attack from goblins and Wargs convinces them to **join forces to defeat evil**. After the battle, Bilbo returns to the comforts of his home, but nothing will be the same now he has tasted such adventure.

3-Second Quest
As the story progresses, the themes and cast open up for Tolkien, suggesting the grand ambitions that would be fulfilled in his later works.

Related Thoughts
see also
AN UNEXPECTED PARTY
page 68
MONSTERS
page 88

❝ *[Smaug's] rage passes description—the sort of rage that is only seen when rich folk that have more than they can enjoy suddenly lose something that they have long had but have never before used or wanted.* **❞**
THE HOBBIT

Smaug the
Magnificent,
from a Russian
edition of
The Hobbit

Bilbo and the World

An instant classic

Initial criticism of Tolkien's first book was positive, some critics even immediately placing *The Hobbit* in the sphere of **great children's books**. It was compared to such works as Edwin A. Abbott's *Flatland*, George MacDonald's *Phantastes*, Lewis Carroll's *Alice's Adventures in Wonderland*, and Kenneth Grahame's *The Wind in the Willows*. For the latter, C. S. Lewis in particular drew parallels between **Bilbo Baggins and Mole**, drawing attention to their prosaic nature and their symbolism of a rural ideal. *The Hobbit* was always **very much a book for children**, more so than the much darker stories of Middle-earth that went into making *The Lord of the Rings* and *The Silmarillion*.

An unlikely hero

A few critics made the point that *The Hobbit* does not try to overwhelm readers by taking them to plains too distant to relate to. Thematically the story is concerned with the **issues that face our own world**, and Tolkien was nothing if not human. He had experienced loss, failure, and, most significantly perhaps, the horrors of the **First World War**, all of which informed his creations and **mythology**. He knew the depths to which human experience could sink, but he also knew the heights to which human endeavor could soar. In Bilbo Baggins, Tolkien had created a character who could carry on his shoulders a great deal of the **author's own worries**, beliefs, and dreams.

Expanding the story

Although the book was woven into the mythology that Tolkien was building in *The Silmarillion* and connected works throughout his life, *The Hobbit* was always meant to be **a standalone work**. The story's success, however, put pressure on its author to create something in the same vein for his next book. Tolkien had created a problem for himself, initially, in that he had given birth to **strikingly memorable characters**. He felt that their story had been told, but it would soon become clear that he needed to explore the **world of Middle-earth** and its characters further. Never meaning *The Hobbit* to have a sequel, Tolkien could certainly never have dreamed of the epic that would come from it.

3-Second Quest
Although Tolkien never had any intention of a sequel for *The Hobbit*, its success and the popularity of its central character meant that some sort of sequel became inevitable.

Related Thoughts
see also
WRITING *THE HOBBIT*
page 48
SUCCESS
page 56

❝ *Seventeen years ago there appeared, without any fanfare, a book called The Hobbit which in my opinion, is one of the best children's stories of this century.* **❞**

W. H. AUDEN,
NEW YORK TIMES, 1954

The "Sequel"

More hobbits, please

Tolkien showed Stanley Unwin various suggestions for a **second book**, and the publisher recognized how promising they were. However, he quickly came to the conclusion that the only sensible option was to build on the success of the adventures of **Bilbo Baggins**. Such was the popularity of his creation, Tolkien agreed, sympathizing with his publisher's point of view. However, he was also determined to publish his detailed history of the **mythology of Middle-earth**— *The Silmarillion*. Ultimately, he would produce a book forged in his mythological world but also featuring the adventures of hobbits: *The Lord of the Rings*.

A creator of worlds

The Silmarillion, on the advice of Unwin, was mined to provide the world and mythology and the foundations for the adventures of Frodo Baggins and *The Fellowship of the Ring*. Tolkien was a **painstaking composer**, and much of the time writing *The Lord of the Rings* was taken up creating the elven language, fashioning the names of the characters so that they had roots etymologically traceable to the **mythological cultures** from which they had purportedly evolved. Tolkien, driven by that obsessive love for myth and language that had held him since childhood, began constructing a world of startling complexity. For instance, the descriptions of the fortifications of Helm's Deep progressed in detail from draft to draft, and he wrote four versions of the hobbit **Merry's lecture on pipe-weed**.

The journey to publication

Tolkien completed *The Lord of the Rings* in the **summer of 1948**—12 years after the release of *The Hobbit*. The years had encompassed revisions and tangents and some periods of complete creative inertia. The journey to publication, in keeping with the **hardships of the characters** within, was an arduous one in itself. But what Tolkien had in his finished manuscript was a single adventure that not only incorporated the mythologies and languages that he had been working on his whole life but also fulfilled the **hunger of the reading public** for fantasy worlds of depth and imagination. Tolkien had, in the minds of many, rendered *The Hobbit*—a work that was never intended to have a sequel—a precursor to his masterpiece.

3-Second Quest
As Tolkien began to write the further adventures of the hobbits of the Shire, the story expanded and expanded into an epic that ultimately took 12 years to write.

Related Thoughts
see also
THE TRILOGY
page 54
THE ALL-CONQUERING FRODO
page 82

❝ *I wonder how could he have been able to invent all this stuff. It feels more like Tolkien discovered some sort of long-lost scrolls.* **❞**

PETER JACKSON, RADIO INTERVIEW, 2001

The Fellowship of the Ring

Disappearing tricks

The Lord of the Rings begins with Bilbo Baggins reaching his **"eleventy-first" birthday**. During the celebrations, which the whole Shire attends, Bilbo announces that he is to leave. Placing the magic ring on his finger, he disappears and heads back to his home, **Bag End**. Gandalf, who witnesses this trick, suspects the ring is more powerful than everyone believes. He places the ring in the care of Bilbo's nephew, Frodo, and also leaves. Several years pass before Gandalf returns to the Shire, having confirmed his fear that the ring is, in fact, the **One Ring of the Dark Lord**, Sauron, forged to rule the people of Middle-earth.

The forming of the Fellowship

Gandalf informs Frodo that he and the Shire are in great danger—Sauron has dispatched the Black Riders to retrieve the Ring. **Frodo leaves the Shire** with his friend and gardener Samwise Gamgee, cousin Peregrin (Pippin) Took, and friend Meriadoc (Merry) Brandybuck for the elven stronghold of Rivendell. Along the way they are **pursued by the Black Riders**. They meet and are protected by a Ranger from the north who reveals himself as Aragorn, son of Arathorn. Once safe in Rivendell, they meet with Gandalf. It is decided that a **Fellowship be formed** consisting of the four hobbits; Aragorn, son of the Steward, heir to the throne of Gondor; Boromir, a man of Gondor; a Dwarf, Gimli; an Elf, Legolas; and, of course, Gandalf himself.

The Fellowship splits

The nine travel south intending to destroy the Ring by casting it into the fires of **Mount Doom** where it was forged, deep in the realm of Sauron's kingdom of Mordor. On the journey they **encounter many dangers**, and when fighting a Balrog, Gandalf falls into a seemingly bottomless pit. Without the wizard, the Fellowship continues until Boromir, under the corrupting power of the Ring, tries to steal it. As a result, Frodo and Sam split from the group and **venture to Mordor** alone. Boromir grows deeply repentant for his actions, and during a ferocious attack from Sauron's Orcs, is killed trying to protect Merry and Pippin. The two hobbits are taken captive.

3-Second Quest
The first book in *The Lord of the Rings* portrays a swift and difficult journey for the young hobbit Frodo, from naïve nephew to the stoic bearer of the great burden of the Ring.

Related Thoughts
see also
THE TRILOGY
page 54
THE TWO TOWERS
page 78

❝ Many that live deserve death. And some that die deserve life. Can you give it to them? Then do not be too eager to deal out death in judgement. For even the very wise cannot see all ends. **❞**

GANDALF,
THE FELLOWSHIP OF THE RING

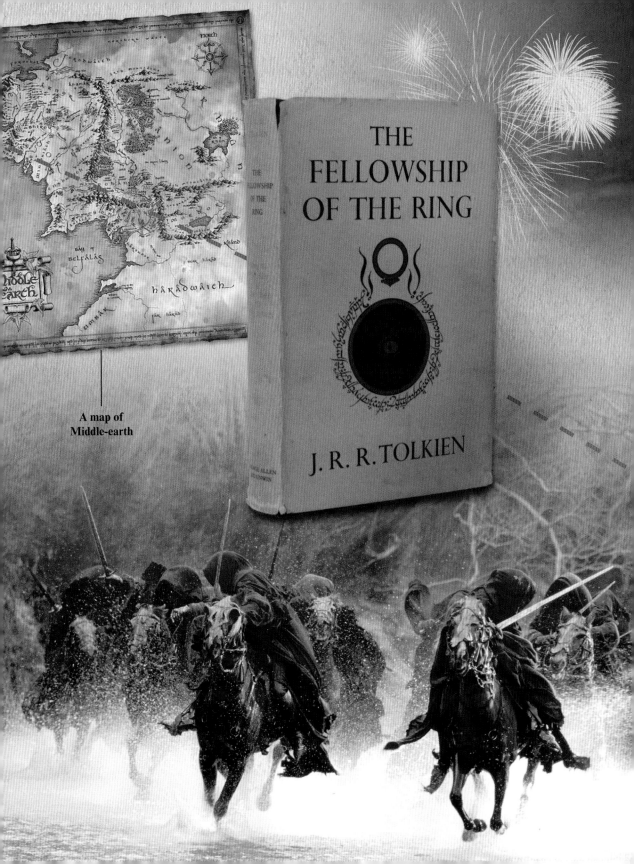

A map of Middle-earth

THE
FELLOWSHIP
OF THE RING

J. R. R. TOLKIEN

The Two Towers

Reunited

Realizing that Frodo and Sam must now **complete their mission alone**, the remaining members of the Fellowship set off in pursuit of Merry and Pippin. They run deep into the heart of the land of Rohan, the realm of the horse lords, and encounter Éomer, the nephew of the king of Rohan. Merry and Pippin escape into Fangorn Forest and the **protection of Treebeard**, the oldest of the Ents—an ancient race of tree guardians who are half Man and half tree. As Aragorn, Gimli, and Legolas pursue the hobbits into the wood, they are reunited with Gandalf, who has been transformed into **Gandalf the White** after his epic battle with the Balrog.

The Battle for Helm's Deep

Gandalf, Aragorn, Gimli, and Legolas ride to the city of Edoras in Rohan to warn King Théoden that Sauron is intent on **destroying the world of Men**. Once there, they free the king from the spell cast over him by his counsel, Gríma Wormtongue, who is an agent of the **evil wizard Saruman**. Saruman, who is in league with Sauron, is creating an army of Orcs in their tens of thousands to march upon Rohan. Here the story truly opens up, and the war for Middle-earth begins with the Battle of Helm's Deep—the fortress reserve of the people of Rohan. With a late intervention from Gandalf, who had gathered reinforcements, the **forces of good are victorious**.

Gollum's return

Meanwhile, Frodo and Sam continue their **long and arduous journey** to Mount Doom. They are joined by the creature Gollum, who has been searching for and following the Ring ever since Bilbo Baggins escaped with it all those years before. Gollum swears on the Ring, his "Precious," that he will guide the two hobbits to Mordor. Instead, he leads them to the **lair of Shelob** (an ancient evil in the form of a giant spider) in the hope of taking the Ring from Frodo's corpse. Frodo is stung into catatonia by the monster, and while Sam fights off the giant spider, **Frodo is abducted by Orcs**. The book ends with the shadow of Sauron forming over Middle-earth, and Frodo, the hope of all, in the hands of the enemy.

3-Second Quest
In the second book, the story opens up and the themes darken and broaden. The narrative incorporates love stories, personal struggles, and epic, sweeping battles.

Related Thoughts
see also
THE FELLOWSHIP OF THE RING
page 76
THE RETURN OF THE KING
page 80

❝ *The counsel of Gandalf was not founded on foreknowledge of safety, for himself or for others,' said Aragorn. 'There are some things that it is better to begin than to refuse, even though the end may be dark.'* **❞**

THE TWO TOWERS

Gandalf returns ———

THE TWO
TOWERS

J. R. R. TOLKIEN

The Return of the King

The battle for Minas Tirith

Gandalf and Pippin ride to Minas Tirith, the chief city of Gondor, in order to rouse the Steward, Denethor, to battle. Aragorn, Gimli, and Legolas travel a different way in order to raise **an army from the ghosts of the dead Men** in the mountains who owe an oath of allegiance to the throne of Gondor to which Aragorn is heir. Along with Faramir (Boromir's brother) and his troops, the forces of Men and Elves converge upon Minas Tirith and once again defeat an even **greater army of Sauron**'s than was faced at Helm's Deep. During this battle, the Witch-king, leader of the Ringwraiths, is slain by Éowyn, daughter of Théoden.

The defeat of Sauron

In the hope that Frodo is still heading to Mount Doom, Aragorn and Gandalf create a distraction by leading an assault upon the **Black Gates of Mordor** with the joint forces of Gondor and Rohan. It works, and, while battle ensues at the gate, Frodo and Sam finally reach the Sammath Naur, **the chambers of fire**, on Mount Doom. Fighting a final temptation to keep the Ring for himself, Frodo is attacked by Gollum, who bites off Frodo's finger to steal the Ring. Dancing in exaltation, Gollum falls into the fiery pit and **the Ring is destroyed**. Sauron's Dark Tower collapses, and Mount Doom erupts. The Dark Lord rises from the shadowy earth, but he disintegrates in the wind. The forces of Minas Tirith are, finally, victorious.

The return to the Shire

After much celebration, and Aragorn's coronation to the throne of Gondor, the hobbits return to the Shire. In dismay, they discover that **their beloved land has been taken over** by Sauron's henchmen under the command of Saruman and Wormtongue (released by the Ents after the defeat of Sauron). Ugly buildings have **destroyed much of the landscape**, and crops have been torn up. Frodo, Sam, Merry, and Pippin drive out the evil, and Saruman and Wormtongue are killed. The Shire returns to its serenity. Frodo, however, is **plagued by his wounds** from the adventure and finally takes flight to the eternal plains of the West on an elven ship, accompanied by Gandalf, Bilbo, and the Elves, Lord Elrond and Lady Galadriel.

3-Second Quest
With the ending of the final book of *The Lord of the Rings*, Tolkien drew to a close an adventure to rival the fables he had studied. He had created not just an epic but a whole world.

Related Thoughts
see also
THE TWO TOWERS
page 76
MIDDLE-EARTH
page 94

" Well, here at last, dear friends, on the shores of the Sea comes the end of our fellowship in Middle-earth. Go in peace! I will not say: do not weep; for not all tears are an evil.**"**

FRODO BAGGINS,
THE RETURN OF THE KING

THE
RETURN OF
THE KING

J. R. R. TOLKIEN

The All-Conquering Frodo

Glimpsing a wider world

The Lord of the Rings, since its publication in 1954, has sold more than **100 million copies worldwide**, behind only the Bible and *The Little Red Book* of Mao Zedong. Tolkien could never have envisioned the impact his creation would have upon the world. Its success is largely a testament to its **intricate detail** but also to the possibilities offered by the world he created. For all the elaborate, thoughtful, and painstakingly devised elements of Middle-earth and its inhabitants, one of the significant characteristics (as more than one critic pointed out at the time) is that we glimpse a much wider world. In this way, Middle-earth is fully realized in that it leaves much to the **reader's imagination**.

Many ages of adventure

The adventures that take place in *The Lord of the Rings* are concerned with one specific age, peopled by characters who are fulfilling their destinies and ambitions. The reader is always aware of other **potential adventures** around every corner, and of the villains, evils, and perils of other times, such is the reality of the geography, mythology, and **history of Middle-earth**. Tolkien went much of the way toward as complete a description of the world and its history as one man with one imagination could in one lifetime, not just with *The Lord of the Rings*, but also with *The Hobbit*, *The Silmarillion*, and the many other texts that went on to be "tidied up," finished, and **published in the years after his death**.

The themes

Tolkien tapped in to many concerns of the modern world with *The Lord of the Rings*, much more so than with *The Hobbit*. As well as notions of duty, of friendship, and of **good versus evil**, Tolkien tackled many more complex ideas including corruption, temptation, disloyalty, isolationism, expansionism, and environmentalism. Tolkien's experiences in the **trenches of the Somme** informed his vision of the evil shadows of the Dark Lord, and his love of the English countryside contributed to his notions of "good." The world of Middle-earth is so vast and so well devised and realized that it is difficult to evaluate fully the accomplishment of Tolkien's imagination, but its **lasting influence** offers a measure of his achievement.

3-Second Quest
The Lord of the Rings went on to be the greatest-selling work of fiction in history. Its influence is as vast and immeasurable as the landscape and experiences of Middle-earth itself.

Related Thoughts
see also

THE TRILOGY
page 54
MIDDLE-EARTH
page 94

❝ *The prime motive was the desire of a tale-teller to try his hand at a really long story that would hold the attention of readers, amuse them, delight them, and at times maybe excite them or deeply move them.* **❞**

FOREWORD TO THE SECOND EDITION, 1966

Heroes

Men

Many of the heroes in Tolkien's mythologies are from the realm of Men. Aragorn, a **traditional romantic hero** in many ways, appears as an archetypal figure of athletic, dignified, courageous, and wise leadership. Figures such as the brothers Boromir and Faramir, although always redeemed in the end, are defined as much by their weaknesses as by their strengths. For Tolkien, **humankind was deeply flawed**, even in moments where they are striving for virtue, but rarely do people represent pure evil. Foolishness is common, as is cruelty through madness or the poison of power's corruption. It is also important to note that although Tolkien's adventures are **male-dominated**, it is the Lady of Rohan, Éowyn, who kills the Witch-king at the battle of Minas Tirith.

Elves

In Tolkien's stories, Elves are most often figures of exceptional **grace and wisdom** (apart from the villainous Wood-elves of *The Hobbit*). Legolas is an important member of the Fellowship. Lord Elrond is a crucial source of guidance to the hobbits throughout the Middle-earth stories; Arwen provides a key insight into Aragorn's character and his motivations; and Lady Galadriel is significant to Frodo's motivation. **Elves were highly significant** in Tolkien's broader vision. His earliest hero, in fact, was Elrond's father, Eärendil, who has his roots as Eärendel the Evening Star in Tolkien's first long poem. It is the Elves who have a **dominant role** in the moral center of Middle-earth, leaving for the West to bequeath the land to Men.

Gandalf

Gandalf stands tall over everything that happens in *The Hobbit* and *The Lord of the Rings*, even when he is absent from the action. Wizard, warrior, guide, counsel, politician, kingmaker, and spiritual leader, Gandalf unites not only the virtuous characters of the books, but he **binds together the themes**. It is Gandalf who gives the story its initial impetus, selecting Bilbo for the dragon adventure in *The Hobbit*, and it is Gandalf who returns from the dead to rescue the hopes of all Middle-earth with his victorious intervention at Helm's Deep. The notion of Gandalf as **a messianic figure** is less applicable than it is to C. S. Lewis's Aslan, but he does appear as an angelic presence after his reincarnation as the White Wizard.

3-Second Quest
Tolkien's heroes are often notable for their adherence to the virtues of the romantic tradition, but they also incorporate the characteristics of the modern age in which Tolkien lived.

Related Thoughts
see also
THE HOBBIT
page 66
PETER JACKSON'S
THE HOBBIT
page 128

" J. R. R. Tolkien's epic trilogy remains the ultimate quest, the ultimate battle between good and evil, the ultimate chronicle of stewardship of the earth. Endlessly imitated, it never has been surpassed. **"**
JOHN MARK EBERHART,
KANSAS CITY STAR, 2000

Gandalf arriving in a
city, from a Russian
edition of *The Hobbit*

Villains

The Dark Lord

Tolkien's compelling depiction of evil is encapsulated in Sauron, whose mythology stretches back to the dawn of time. **Sauron was one of the original beings** of the creators, the Ainur, but he sided with the first Dark Lord, Morgoth, in the rebellion of the Elder Days. After Morgoth's defeat, Sauron began imitating his master and marched an army upon the free peoples of Middle-earth. Using the One Ring of Power that he had secretly forged in the fires of Mount Doom, he **enslaved the most powerful army of Men**, the Númenóreans, nine of whom he bound as his servants—the fearsome Nazgûl (or Ringwraiths). Sauron **ruled Middle-earth** for much of the Second Age until Isuldur and a surviving Númenórean army defeated him, Isuldur cutting the Ruling Ring from Sauron's hand.

Servants of Sauron

Throughout the ages, Sauron's dark power preyed mercilessly on the weakminded and turned them to his service. Of the race of wizards, Sauron corrupted **Saruman the White**, who was tempted by the power he could wield at the Dark Lord's side. But aside from agents such as the **Nazgûl** and **Gríma Wormtongue**, the power of the Ring commanded an enormous army—Orcs. These servants lacked all moral attributes, and in many ways are portrayed by Tolkien as nothing more than wild animals in humanoid form. Part of their terror lies in their abundance in the **armies of Sauron and Saruman**, bringing shadows to Middle-earth in their tens of thousands. Critics have seen in this echoes of the industrialization of the English countryside that was a predominant concern of Tolkien's.

Gollum

Gollum's story is tragic rather than villainous. Only briefly, while he is in his original incarnation as the hobbit, **Sméagol**, do we see him free from the corrupting influence of the Ring. He then murders his cousin Déagol for possession of it. Ostracized by his village, Sméagol, by then named Gollum, retreats underground in the Misty Mountains where, over hundreds of years, the **Ring's power distorts his mind and body**. Gollum, ultimately, is essential to Frodo and Sam reaching Mount Doom, and he is a pathetic counterpoint to the commanding power of Sauron. His relationship to the Ring and schizophrenic personality are central to the tale of power, good, and evil. Although doomed, Gollum is one of the only villains who approaches any form of **redemption**.

3-Second Quest

Tolkien creates a complex mythology of evil, which seeps from the Dark Lord Sauron through the corrupting power of the Ring to distort the nature of figures such as Gollum.

Related Thoughts

see also
THE TWO TOWERS
page 78
MONSTERS
page 88

❝ Sauron's lust and pride increased, until he knew no bounds, and he determined to make himself master of all things in Middle-earth. **❞**

THE SILMARILLION

The Dark Riders

Gollum

Monsters

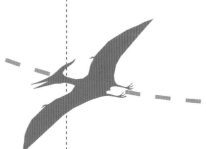

Ancient forces

Whereas many of the monsters in Middle-earth are little more than ferocious animals, such as **Cave Trolls and Wargs**, some of the most significant beings in *The Hobbit* and *The Lord of the Rings* originate from the farthest reaches of time. These monsters are bathed in dark magic and **corrupted celestial powers**. The Balrog, for example, was once a virtuous "angelic" being—a Maiar—who, alongside Sauron, was turned evil and corrupt by the Dark Lord Morgoth. Once a spirit of fire, by the time the Fellowship encounters the last remaining Balrog deep in the mines of Moria, he is a powerful demon of shadow with **dragonlike wings**, a whip of thongs, and a sword of fire.

Myth and monster

Many of the Middle-earth monsters, not surprisingly given Tolkien's scholarship, have roots that can be traced to **established mythologies**, which are then developed into terrifying and original creatures. The "Watcher in the Water," which the Fellowship encounters outside the gates of Moria, has similarities to the **kraken of Norse myth**. Dragons, Trolls, and Orcs can all be traced to myriad ancient mythologies across the world, including Nordic, Oriental, and myths of the Middle East. Of course, all mythologies interweave, and Tolkien's triumph was to create one as dense and complex as classical myths. He was adept at pointing to a **terrifying characteristic** in his monsters, and weaving them convincingly into human stories, then allowing the reader's imagination to do the rest.

The shock of the familiar

The stories of J. R. R. Tolkien are placed in a world that seems familiar to us, juxtaposed with the unfamiliar and the **supernatural** that lurks around every corner. As we have seen, Tolkien never meant Middle-earth to be an alien planet, and he was careful to **locate his monsters in a mythology** and a landscape that built upon the traditions and fears of our own land. Monsters such as the Nazgûl hark back to **prehistoric times**, while the enormous size of creatures such as the spider Shelob, Wargs, and Oliphaunts is imagined to weave around familiar fears. It is the close relationship to the familiar that can make Tolkien's monsters as disturbing and as believable as they are.

3-Second Quest
Tolkien's monsters, varied as they are, always have solid roots, not only in the mythologies of ancient and medieval civilizations but also in the creatures of the modern world.

Related Thoughts
see also
THE TRILOGY
page 54
VILLAINS
page 86

❝*Evil labors with vast power and perpetual success, but in vain, preparing always only the soil for unexpected good to sprout in.*❞
THE LETTERS OF J.R.R. TOLKIEN

Mythology

Ancient beginnings

Tolkien's work draws upon many of his life's influences, from **the Bible** to the medieval romances and myth cycles to which he was dedicated. From the punitive flooding of the island of Númenór at the end of the Second Age to the **apocalyptic horsemen**, it is easy to find biblical inspiration. But for the most part Tolkien's Legendarium (as he termed it) falls strongly into the romantic tradition, drawing on the Anglo-Saxon poem *Beowulf* and the Finnish and Nordic sagas. Doomed love, ethereal but earthly magic, and, perhaps most strikingly, the clear delineation of good versus evil are clear themes. Tolkien drew upon his life's work to create a series of legends that possess all the power of **classical mythology**.

3-Second Quest
The legends, folk songs, poems, and, most importantly, the languages that Tolkien created gave his writing a unique sense of depth and authority.

Poetry and song

Tolkien's first foray into the telling of legends was his poetry, and he wrote a great many **narrative epics** telling the stories of his created myths. From "The Voyage of Eärendil the Evening Star" to the popular romance "The Tale of Beren and Lúthien," most of these tales fed into the mythologies of Middle-earth and became important legends. Tom Bombadil stepped out from his **poetic beginnings** and became an important character in the early part of *The Lord of the Rings*. Both *The Hobbit* and *The Lord of the Rings* on publication were immediately distinct from other fantasy fiction for their incorporation of poems and **folk songs** into the text. This added to the complexity and authenticity of Tolkien's world.

Related Thoughts
see also
STUDYING MYTHS
page 32
TEACHER AND SCHOLAR
page 40

Languages

Tolkien believed that the eye into the soul of a people was the language they used, and he spent a great deal of creative energy on the development and **intricate constructions** of his own elaborate languages. One might even argue that his stories were on some level a way for Tolkien to publish and display these, his favorite creations. From the **elvish languages of Quenderin** and their myriad offshoots, to the Khuzdul language of the Dwarves, to the Black Speech spoken in Mordor, Tolkien built full and elaborate explanations of how languages were **passed down through the ages**. Rather than giving languages to his created races, Tolkien saw the histories, traditions, beliefs, and behaviors of his peoples as deriving from their languages.

❝ *Fantasy remains a human right: we make in our measure and in our derivative mode, because we are made: and not only made, but made in the image and likeness of a Maker.* **❞**
ON FAIRY-STORIES

Magic and Religion

The nature of evil

In Tolkien's Middle-earth, "evil" is a complex notion and is not, as some may suggest, symbolized by cipher characters and shadows of **pathetic fallacy**. Sauron, as the greatest example of Tolkien's idea of evil, has a long, turbulent, and varied personal history that stretches out to the beginning of Middle-earth's creation. A **corrupted celestial warrior**, his journey reflects in many ways that of the angel Lucifer in Christian mythology or, more accurately, a disciple of Lucifer, making Morgoth the devil himself. Sauron was once just, and his journey to becoming the Dark Lord of Mordor is often defined by an absence of good, a particularly **Catholic theological idea**. Much that informs Tolkien's weightier themes appears to come from strongly held Catholic beliefs.

Magical powers

Although magic exists in the realms of Middle-earth, Tolkien is careful not to rely on it heavily either as a device to deliver dramatic tension or as a *deus ex machina*. Importantly, not just anyone can **obtain magical powers**—mostly, those with inherent powers are not originally born of Middle-earth. The wizards are celestial, as are the origins of the Elves and Sauron himself. Most other magic is imparted by these **"angelic" figures** who have a direct connection to the creators through spells and powerful items such as the Ring. Thus magic is not a **pagan power**, and neither is it a truly fantastical whim, but rather it has a definite connection to the Old Testament "magic" of Christianity's celestial powers.

Religion, gods, and wizards

Religion and faith are important to the peoples of Middle-earth, although they take many forms. Many races have quasi-pagan beliefs, such as the druidic, agricultural forces in elven and dwarvish faith systems who see the presence of a **supreme power** not in cathedrals but in the earth itself. In the histories of Middle-earth, Tolkien lays out the creation and evolutionary myths that are the fabric of much organized religion. The wizards are certainly **representative of angels**, and like the angels of Christian mythology come in a variety of shapes and sizes. Indeed, it is Gandalf and Saruman who offer the closest things Middle-earth has to a gnostic theological strand, as **"gods" who have taken an earthly form**.

3-Second Quest
As important as religion and faith were to J. R. R. Tolkien, it is only the careful reader who can identify strands of his Catholicism in his fiction.

Related Thoughts
see also
SCHOOL YEARS
page 24
MYTHOLOGY
page 90

❝I don't feel under any obligation to make my story fit with formalized Christian theology, though I actually intended it to be consonant with Christian thought and belief.**❞**

THE LETTERS OF J.R.R. TOLKIEN

Middle-earth

A land not so far away

When Tolkien began to create his alternate mythologies, languages, and worlds, he not only used the legends of those cultures dear to him for inspiration, but also adapted a **familiar landscape**. Middle-earth is in fact our own Earth at a distant time when the geography and topography are quite different but not alien. The flora and fauna are the same as ours; giant creatures such as **eagles and Oliphaunts** may be magical, but we can see their relatives in our own world. Middle-earth has a vast, complex mythological history, spanning thousands and thousands of years, but it is still earth. *The Lord of the Rings* tells a story that marks the **burgeoning of the age of Man**.

Maps

Tolkien was a skilful creator of maps and his cartography formed an ornate and colorful cornerstone for his books, drawing on his considerable artistic abilities. He believed that **a map gave birth to a people**, just as he believed a language could give birth to a culture and give a nature and behavior to that culture. Tolkien had drawn maps from an early age, but the most significant in his evolution as a storyteller was **Thror's Map**, for some time the only addition to the composition of the opening line from *The Hobbit*. In the 1930s Tolkien **spent much time and effort** creating maps of his world; eventually his son Christopher compiled them into a volume called *The Shaping of Middle-earth*, published in 1986.

Diverse realms

The realms of Middle-earth, each dominated by a chief town, were very much tribal regions, and there seems to be little room for multicultural centers. All tightly bound to their **etymological root**, Tolkien fashioned complex tales of the histories of these places: the lands of Men, such as Gondor and Rohan; Rivendell and Lothlórien for the Elves; Isengard becoming a dark, corrupt land where Saruman raises the Dark Lord's armies; Moria the Dwarf city; **the Shire of the hobbits**; and Mordor, the bastion of Sauron. There are many, many others. The geography of these realms reflects the nature of the peoples who inhabit them, through such tropes as the **Gothic tower of Cirith Ungol** or the ethereal woodlands of Lothlórien.

3-Second Quest
Middle-earth, although filled with monsters and magical beings, was never designed as an alien planet, but rather it is the world in which the world we know began.

Related Thoughts
see also
OXFORD
page 30
CONSERVATION AND LANDSCAPE
page 148

❝ Part of the attraction is, I think, due to the glimpses of a large history in the background: an attraction like that of viewing far off an unvisited island, or seeing the towers of a distant city gleaming in a sunlit mist. **❞**

THE LETTERS OF J.R.R. TOLKIEN

The Silmarillion

Mythopoeia

In many ways Tolkien's most important work, the book that he began in his youth and remained working on throughout his life, is *The Silmarillion*. This **collection of legends** marks the basis for the majority of his writings and was the conduit through which he conceived and produced his own worlds, languages, and mythologies. At first called the "**legendarium**," Tolkien used it to coin a term, "mythopoeia," in which a writer devises and constructs entire mythological histories. *The Silmarillion* is as vast and complete a mythopoeic vision as any one man has produced. The stories that make up the volume equate to **the history of Middle-earth**—its wars and romances, its birth, its cultures, and its final fade.

A tumultuous history

The Silmarillion contains some of Tolkien's most popular tales, including the romance of Beren and Lúthien, and **the voyage of Eärendil**. The book is split into five sections, each detailing a history of Middle-earth, from its creation to the end of the Third Age, with Sauron's defeat and the beginning of the Age of Men. The largest section, the Quenta Silmarillion, reports **the theft of the Silmarils** (three magical elven jewels) by the Dark Lord Melkor (later Morgoth), seducer of both Sauron and the Balrog into darkness. The resultant war between the dark forces and free peoples formed **the union of Elves and Men**, and a long cast-out light returned to Middle-earth. Tolkien's legendarium is the context in which Frodo's adventure plays out.

The compilation of the tales

Although Tolkien began what would become *The Silmarillion* in 1914, he did not finish the work. It was left to his son, **Christopher**, to compile the wealth of scattered notes and stories into a narrative. What Christopher achieved was nothing short of remarkable—sometimes creating entire narrative strands from scratch to **make a smooth journey across the ages**. However, *The Silmarillion* is regarded as a minor work of fiction in comparison to *The Lord of the Rings* and *The Hobbit*—a fabulous backdrop to the other more popular stories. It lacks a truly heroic central quest or iconic characters such as Frodo or Gandalf, but it offers the dedicated reader an impressive means to fully **explore the riches of Tolkien's imagined world**.

3-Second Quest
The Silmarillion, although not as critically or commercially successful as *The Lord of the Rings* or *The Hobbit*, is the context for both. Neither volume would exist without it.

Related Thoughts
see also
THE HOBBIT
page 66
THE 'SEQUEL'
page 74

❝*It is not our part to master all the tides of the world, but to do what is in us for the succour of those years wherein we are set.***❞**

THE RETURN OF THE KING

Shorter Works

Farmer Giles of Ham

Published in 1949, Tolkien's **short fable about a farmer** who enjoys a series of encounters with the dragon, Chrysophylax, offers a fascinating insight into the author's early ideas and interpretations of romantic sagas. It is a **cheerful, lighthearted tale** in which Farmer Giles rises from humble beginnings to become a rival to the king. *Farmer Giles of Ham* takes place in medieval Britain, albeit a fantastical version, and is closer, perhaps, to the Arthurian cycle of Malory than it is to Tolkien's own Middle-earth legendarium. Although it is **very much a children's story** and contains none of the darkness and weighty themes of even *The Hobbit*, it is an early signal toward the epic works that Tolkien would later create.

The Adventures of Tom Bombadil

Tom Bombadil is an intriguing character who offers a thread through different Tolkien works. He is **one of the oldest creatures** in the Middle-earth pantheon—a spirit who symbolizes but also helps define the spirit of nature. The Elves believe him to be an incarnation of the **ancient life force of the forest**. He appears first in the poem "The Adventures of Tom Bombadil," which Tolkien wrote for his children. This poem eventually **becomes a hobbit folk song**. Bombadil is most closely associated with *The Lord of the Rings*, not only as he appears in the first book (where Frodo and his hobbit travelers encounter him on their journey to Rivendell) but also in the tone he sets for the journey.

Smith of Wootton Major

Originally asked to write an introduction to the **fairy stories of George MacDonald**, Tolkien instead wrote this tale, which is designed to ridicule the idea that fairy stories were for children. *Smith of Wootton Major* is dark and heavy, written by Tolkien when he was in his 70s, and it is delivered in the **sad, reserved, and gracious tone** adopted by a writer closer to the end of his life than the beginning. Smith of the title finds a magic star hidden in a cake that allows him access to the magical land of Faery. It plays on themes familiar to any reader of Tolkien—magic, duty, destiny, corruption, and folly—but it is striving for something quite different, being **reflective and overtly profound**.

3-Second Quest
Tolkien's shorter works are important to anyone trying to understand Tolkien's journey as a writer, many of them signaling his directions and the place he would arrive at.

Related Thoughts
see also
THE STORIES
page 46
THE CHILDREN'S AUTHOR
page 50

❝ *How do you pick up the threads of an old life? How do you go on, when in your heart, you begin to understand, there is no going back?* **❞**

THE RETURN OF THE KING

The Writer's Concerns

A true niggler

Despite Tolkien's vociferous dislike and distrust of allegory, his story published in the *Dublin Review* in 1945 is often seen as one. "**Leaf by Niggle**," if not an allegory, is certainly a tale grown from Tolkien's experiences and frustrations with his life and work. Niggle (Tolkien often said that he was a "niggler," obsessing over every line of his work), an artist, paints a great tree, in the background of which is a forest. **Niggle obsesses over each leaf**, attending to its unique detail. Soon, all of his other work is either abandoned or absorbed into this great project. All the while Niggle is **distracted by the chores of mundane everyday life**, until he realizes he will never complete his painting.

Terrific tales

Published long after Tolkien's death in 1982, *Mr. Bliss* was the **illustrated children's story** he wrote in the 1930s. Mr. Bliss is a hilariously dangerous driver, much as Tolkien himself was, and also recalling Mr. Toad in Kenneth Grahame's classic 1908 children's novel *The Wind in the Willows*. The story portrays the adventures of the titular character in his new automobile as he creates general disorder and mayhem, angering shopkeepers, neighbors, and even a bear. Tolkien wrote many such short stories that have **very little in common with the works that made his name**. They include *Roverandom*, the story of an inquisitive dog turned into a toy by a wizard, and the fabulous *Father Christmas Letters*, which brought together the detailed tales Tolkien wrote in the annual letter he sent every Christmas Eve to his children from Father Christmas.

Striking the right note

Throughout Tolkien's work, from the vastness of *The Silmarillion*, through the breathless adventure and depth of *The Lord of the Rings*, to the slightness and lightness of *Mr. Bliss*, the **themes remain the same**. Tolkien is concerned with his own ideas of humankind's place, how we should not consider ourselves either alone or special in the world, and how nature has a right to exist not subserviently but alongside us. Tolkien is not only regarded nowadays as **the father of modern fantasy** but also as a proto-environmentalist, often expressing radical ideas through the mouths of characters such as Ents, Elves, and hobbits. As his greatest works were published in paperback in the 1960s, these themes struck chords with **a vibrant, aware, literate, and activist youth**.

3-Second Quest

Not everything Tolkien wrote was centered on Middle-earth, or even bore the mark of medieval Nordic mythologies, and some of his children's stories were quite different and playful.

Related Thoughts

see also

THE STORIES
page 46
SHORTER WORKS
page 98

❝ All tales may come true; and yet, at the last, redeemed, they may be as like and unlike the forms that we give them as Man, finally redeemed, will be like and unlike the fallen that we know. **❞**

ON FAIRY-STORIES

Mr. Toad

Tolkien at home in
his study

The Academic

Scholarly works

Tolkien was first and foremost an academic, and a very successful one at that. Along with C. S. Lewis, he went some way to **reinventing the public perception** of his hitherto rather dry area of expertise, using his popular fantasies as a window into the exciting world of folklore and European mythology. His supreme **excellence in the languages of the Middle Ages** greatly informed the array of languages he created for Middle-earth, and his knowledge of some of the great works of long ago, such as *Beowulf* and *Sir Gawain and the Green Knight*, fed into the romances and adventures of his own mythologies. Beyond the boundaries of Middle-earth, **Tolkien wrote significant essays**, lectures, and translations around these texts.

Beowulf

Tolkien's famous lecture and essay, "Beowulf: The Monsters and the Critics," completely changed the way the poem was studied, **shifting the academic focus** from the historical relevance of the text to its literary significance. Tolkien was a great admirer of the poem, believing it **an eminent work of English literature** that should be discussed in the terms reserved for Chaucer or Shakespeare rather than as a relic. The story tells of the hero Beowulf who rids a town of persecution by the creature Grendel. The poem informed his fantastical writing, from the **particular homage to it** with Bilbo's theft from Smaug in *The Hobbit* to the philological connection between Beorn, the shapeshifter encountered by Bilbo and his retinue, and the hero Beowulf himself.

Sir Gawain and the Green Knight

In 1953 Tolkien was invited to give the prestigious W. P. Ker lecture at **Glasgow University**, and he presented it on *Sir Gawain and the Green Knight*. In many ways the adventure of Sir Gawain encompasses many of the most important themes in Tolkien's work. It has the chivalrous characteristic of its hero, a quest, and obvious ecological overtones. It also **possesses a tangible darkness and brutality** that was common to myths of this age but, as Tolkien felt, had been lost in the fantasy works of the nineteenth and twentieth centuries. The tale is a complex one, and it is difficult to clearly separate the "hero" from the "villain." Tolkien's translation was **sufficiently masterful** that it has become the standard text.

3-Second Quest
Tolkien was an esteemed scholar in the field of philology and English, but his academic passions were never far removed from his fiction.

Related Thoughts
see also
TEACHER AND SCHOLAR
page 40
SUCCESS
page 56

ff *Folk-tales... do often contain elements that are thin and cheap, with little even potential virtue; but they also contain much that is far more powerful, and that cannot be sharply separated from myth.* **"**
BEOWULF: THE MONSTERS AND THE CRITICS, 1934

Glasgow University,
Scotland

After Tolkien

Delving into Middle-earth's history

After J. R. R. Tolkien's death in 1973, his family (in particular his son Christopher) began **arranging his unpublished works**. A series of books were published, collectively known as *The History of Middle-earth*. The first, *The Book of Lost Tales : 1*, was published in 1983, with the final volume in the series, *The People of Middle-earth*, appearing in 1996. The 12 books are made up not just of stories built up from **Tolkien manuscripts in various states of completion** but are also filled with informative glossaries, maps, and quasi-sociological documents about the inhabitants of Middle-earth. Although awkwardly received by critics on the whole, the books are **a fascinating insight** not only into Middle-earth but into the mind of Tolkien himself.

Christopher Tolkien

Tolkien's youngest son, Christopher, has **worked tirelessly** to ensure that his father's work meets readers in a way that his father, the perfectionist "niggler," could not have done. Toward the end of his life, Tolkien had come to terms with the fact that *The Silmarillion* would never be published, but Christopher brought it to print after **years of painstaking work** on the manuscript. As well as this success, he toiled over the enormous collection of his father's papers to create *The History of Middle-earth* and, more recently, collections of his father's poetry. In 2007 he produced the book *The Children of Húrin* and in 2009 the poem *The Legend of Sigurd and Gudrún*. Christopher has in many ways kept the wonders of Middle-earth growing.

A modern influence

J. R. R. Tolkien's influence upon the world of fantasy cannot be undervalued—he is **the father of the entire modern industry**. He changed the way that writers approached the subject, showed that fantasy could be written for adults as well as children by **addressing universal themes without being allegorical**, created modern characters in ancient settings, and elicited true emotional involvement for the reader. The genre itself had been archaic and meager before *The Lord of the Rings*, and although Tolkien himself is guilty of archaisms in his work and style, his legacy could not be more modern. The vastness of his creation means that there are **no limits to the genre**, and he has arguably had an even greater influence on the entertainment industry than he has on literature.

3-Second Quest
The work of Tolkien has enjoyed a whole new existence in the decades since his death, with a library of unpublished works coming forward to influence the fantasy industry.

Related Thoughts
see also
OXFORD LIFE
page 44
ENDURING POPULARITY
page 112

❝I am personally immensely amused by hobbits as such, and can contemplate them eating and making their rather fatuous remarks indefinitely; but I find that is not the case with even my most devoted fans.**❞**
THE LETTERS OF J.R.R. TOLKIEN

Timeline

1915
Publishes first poem in professional anthology, "Goblin Feet," in *Oxford Poetry*, 1915. It was a poem he soon despised.

1922
A well-respected academic work, *A Middle English Vocabulary* is published in Oxford by Clarendon Press.

1925
In collaboration with E. V. Gordon, Tolkien publishes a translation of *Sir Gawain and the Green Knight*.

1933
The *Oxford Magazine* publishes "Errantry"—a poem that eventually becomes "The Lady of Eärendil" in the second book of *The Lord of the Rings*.

1934
The poem "The Adventures of Tom Bombadil" is printed in the *Oxford Magazine*. This starts a prolific publishing burst of mythopoeic poems about Middle-earth.

1936
Without Tolkien's approval, a group of students publish his "Song for the Philologists," a comic verse that he and his colleagues had written.

1937
In the same year that Tolkien publishes *The Hobbit*, his essay from his influential lecture "*Beowulf: The Monsters and the Critics*" is printed.

1945
"Leaf by Niggle," a short, serious work, is published in the *Dublin Review*.

1949

Farmer Giles of Ham is published.

1954-55

Published in three volumes over the period of a year *The Lord of the Rings* is released in the UK and in the USA.

1962

A book titled *The Adventures of Tom Bombadil* is published collating much of the Middle-earth verse and folk songs.

1967

The Road Goes Ever On: A Song Cycle brought together the poems of J. R. R. Tolkien and the music of Donald Swann. *Smith of Wootton Major* is also published.

1976

Just a few years after Tolkien's death, with the editorial supervision of his son Christopher, *The Father Christmas Letters* are published, anthologizing the imaginative letters Tolkien wrote for his children each year when they were young.

1977

After a painstaking curation, Christopher Tolkien creates a satisfying manuscript, and *The Silmarillion*, his father's labor of love, is finally published.

1982

Tolkien's charming children's tale, *Mr. Bliss*, is published with his own original illustrations.

1983

The Book of Lost Tales: Part One sees the beginning of the compilations and publication by Christopher Tolkien of *The History of Middle-earth*.

Glossary

Balrog Morgoth twisted this ancient maiar spirit into a terrible demon. It breathed flame and had a whip of fire.

Black Riders The greatest of Sauron's servants, they were also called Nazgûl ("Ring-wraiths"). These nine wraiths were once men who had each been given a Ring of Power that was ruled by Sauron's One Ring.

dragons The most powerful demons created by Morgoth. A winged fire-breathing dragon called Smaug wrought terror on the Dwarf-kingdom.

Dwarves A race of strong and stout miners and craftspeople of around four to five feet in height.

Elves A strong, fair people who do not age, but grow wiser and fairer. Elven kingdoms are found in the forests of Mirkwood and Lothlórien, and in the valley of Rivendell.

Ents Ancient forest giants 14-feet tall who are half Men and half trees. They stand guard over the trees of Fangorn Forest.

Goblins Evil servants of the Dark Lord Sauron; also known as Orcs.

Hobbits Also called halflings, these small people (between two to four feet high) are long-fingered and cheerful, with large, hairy feet. They live in the Shire.

Maiar These ancient holy beings include wizards and creatures that were corrupted by Morgoth, including the Balrogs and Sauron.

Morgoth One of the mightiest beings, called Valar, who first came to live on the world when it was created. Morgoth was the first Dark Lord.

Nazgûl See Black Riders.

Orcs The race of Orcs were once Elves, but were enslaved through torture. They had cold, black blood, and obeyed their master (the Dark Lord Sauron).

Shelob A giant spider demon whose offspring live in Mirkwood and Mordor. Shelob lived in Cirith Ungol until she was killed by Sam Gamgee.

Smaug the Magnificent A winged, fire-breathing dragon that lived in the Misty Mountains. He was killed with a single arrow.

Trolls A race of giant cannibals with green, scaly skin. They can be turned to stone by sunlight.

Wargs Evil, giant wolves that had an alliance with Orcs, who rode them like horses.

Witch-king The Lord of the Nazgûl who was originally a sorcerer. He was killed by Éowyn, Lady of Rohan.

wizards Ancient and powerful Maiar spirits who took the form of Men.

Chapter 3

Influence

Enduring Popularity

Father of Fantasy

When considering the influence of J. R. R Tolkien, one must surely start with the extraordinary impact of *The Lord of the Rings*. Tolkien, with his mythopoeic approach to fantasy, **changed the landscape** and possibilities not just of modern literature but of many other aspects of modern popular culture. Not for nothing is Tolkien known as the "Father of Fantasy." Had he written no book other than *The Hobbit*, he might simply have been remembered as the writer of a curious and extremely popular children's story. But *The Lord of the Rings* has an **enduring influence over so many aspects of the entertainment industry**, from books and movies to music and theater.

Readers in their millions

Books with global popularity are often subject to debate when it comes to sales figures. But it is estimated that *The Hobbit* and *The Lord of the Rings*, in its three-volume format, have each sold some **150 million copies worldwide**, having been translated into more than **38 languages**. The enormity of the numbers and the disparity of estimates tells its own story. Tolkien's work, in every way from cultural impact to tangible statistics, is impossible to truly grasp. However, we can be sure that the tales Tolkien first devised as bedtime stories for his children have had a **lasting impact on the lives of millions** of readers around the globe.

Awards

The books have won many prizes (most commonly in the field of fantasy—from the **International Fantasy Award in 1957** to the Prometheus Hall of Fame Award in 2009). But adaptations have been equally successful, culminating in **Peter Jackson's domination of the Oscars in 2004** for the conclusion of his movie interpretations of *The Lord of the Rings* trilogy. In 2006 the musical-theater version of *The Lord of the Rings* was nominated for **seven Olivier Awards** in London. But it is with the public that Tolkien's work has always found the most favor, frequently topping favorite book polls, such as the BBC's national poll of 2004, and making appearances in the lists of **greatest books of the century**, keeping the most esteemed literary company.

3-Second Quest
Tolkien's stories of Middle-earth not only went on to be extremely popular, award-winning books but they helped create a whole new industry in publishing.

Related Thoughts
see also
SUCCESS
page 56
THE ALL-CONQUERING FRODO
page 82

❝You step onto the road, and if you don't keep your feet, there's no knowing where you might be swept off to.**❞**
FRODO QUOTING BILBO,
THE FELLOWSHIP OF THE RING

Peter Jackson collects one of the many Oscars awarded to his film adaptations

A Classic Work

Serious literature?

For all of the success and popularity of Tolkien's work, it has often found itself at the center of a common debate: how seriously can fantasy literature be taken? Many of the criticisms of fantasy, that it is childish, nonsense-based, light **escapism**, that it is shallow of thought and composition, can hardly be applied to Tolkien. There has been no more fastidious a writer of fantasy than he. His **greatest successors**, such as those writers of high fantasy George R. R. Martin, Phillip Pulman, and Alan Garner, do not imitate Tolkien but have rather **built upon the foundations** his imagination forged and the infinite possibilities of his creative impulses.

Prestigious recognition

It was recently revealed that C. S. Lewis **nominated Tolkien for the Nobel Prize**, literature's greatest award, in 1961, but the judges discounted Tolkien for his archaic prose style. The award that year, interestingly, went to Yugoslav novelist **Ivo Andric**, whose greatest work was *The Bosnian Trilogy*, a series of books that drew heavily on the folklore of his native Bosnia. Tolkien, however, never seemed to voice concern over the lack of recognition from the literati of his day. Although his work was often savagely reviewed (as well as lovingly reviewed by others), his greatest pleasure was in the **undeniable popularity with readers**, a popularity the influence of his creations proves.

The use of fantasy

Fantasy is not in itself looked down upon by the literati; it is the form that fantasy takes that seems to be problematic. Some of the greatest writers of all time have delivered their message from the shores of fantastical worlds—Jonathan Swift's **Gulliver's Travels** being one potent example. The great literary writers of the twentieth century, from Tolkien's contemporaries such as **George Orwell** to modern masters such as Doris Lessing and Margaret Atwood, would be unlikely to name the author of *The Lord of the Rings* as **their greatest influence**. However, Tolkien's trailblazing use of fantasy opened huge possibilities for literature with his use of alien-but-familiar landscapes and his exploration of relevant themes in fantastical stories.

3-Second Quest
The debate over the seriousness of fantasy will continue, but Tolkien's influence can be felt everywhere, from children's stories to the most respected high-brow literature.

Related Thoughts
see also
THE ACADEMIC
page 102
A GROWING GENRE
page 118

❝ When I grew up... I wanted to write The Lord of the Rings. The problem was that it had already been written. **❞**
NEIL GAIMAN

George Orwell

Gulliver's Travels

Ivo Andric

High Fantasy

The Chronicles of Narnia

Tolkien believed that his great friend C. S. Lewis would never have written *The Chronicles of Narnia* were it not for his own fiction. Lewis was a **great admirer** not only of the work of his friend but of the attitude and processes that Tolkien used in the **construction of his tales**. Lewis was always quite open in paying homage to Tolkien's influence. Tolkien, for his part, disliked Lewis's stories for a number of reasons. He passionately **disapproved of allegory** as a literary form, and the *Chronicles* has certainly been labeled as allegorical; but Tolkien was also uncomfortable with the brevity of Lewis's composition—the seven volumes of *The Chronicles of Narnia* came out in consecutive years between 1950 and 1956.

The worlds of Alan Garner

Alan Garner took up the challenge set by publishers to find the next Tolkien. He produced intelligent fantastical works that seemed to bridge a gap between Tolkien and Lewis both thematically and conceptually. *The Weirdstone of Brisingamen*, published in 1957, was a critical and commercial success, and the first of a trilogy of **fantasy novels** that reached its completion with the publication of *Boneland* in 2012. The story of the **perilous adventures** of two children, Susan and Colin, who with the help of a wizard battle malevolent demons near their country home, Garner's work broadened further the possibilities for imaginative fiction. At the same time, it drew the **fantastical elements** of Tolkien's style even closer to our own world.

Sword and sorcery

Perhaps Tolkien's most significant contribution to literature was his inadvertent creation of the genre now known as "**high fantasy**." The genre's main characteristic is the setting of the story in an alternate world (what Tolkien called "subcreation"), and writers in this area hold Tolkien and Lewis as their patron saints. Also sometimes called **sword-and-sorcery novels**, they can be further subdivided into three types: those where the world is ultimate and our world does not exist (such as George R. R. Martin's *Song of Ice and Fire*); those where the alternate world is reached through a portal from our world (such as Philip Pullman's *His Dark Materials*); and those where the **alternate world is hidden within our own** (such as J. K. Rowling's *Harry Potter* books).

3-Second Quest
Middle-earth inspired and influenced many types of fantasy novel. High fantasy and "subcreation" are part of Tolkien's literary legacy.

Related Thoughts
see also
SUCCESS
page 56
A GROWING GENRE
page 118

❝*Some who have read the book, or at any rate have reviewed it, have found it boring, absurd, or contemptible; and I have no cause to complain, since I have similar opinions of their works.***❞**

THE LORD OF THE RINGS, FOREWORD TO THE SECOND EDITION, 1966

C. S. Lewis ————

A Growing Genre

Not children's books

Many great fantastical works of the twentieth century have been wrongly regarded as children's books simply due to their **fantastical nature**. Astonishingly, this patronizing misconception can be traced as far back as *Gulliver's Travels*, regarded in Victorian England as a fanciful children's story rather than the classic satire that it was. But it is often worth investigating **the feelings of the novelists themselves** rather than the intentions of the publishers. Richard Adams' *Watership Down*, for instance, shares many similarities with Tolkien's work—ecological themes, invented languages, traveling fellowships, a quest, invented mythologies, and not least his testament that his tale of rabbits **looking for their Utopia** should not be treated as a children's story.

Worlds apart

Tolkien's influence can be seen in many works that have gone on to have literary weight and popular success and which are not thought of in the same genre as Tolkien despite being fantasy. **Terry Pratchett's** best-selling *"Discworld"* books are fine examples of **comic fantasy**, and they draw elements of their humor from characters and plots that trace their heritage to Frodo, Gandalf, and the idea of the quest. They are, in Tolkien's tradition, **brilliantly imaginative**. At the other end of the scale are works such as George R. R. Martin's *Song of Ice and Fire*—a dynastic epic set in a world similar to that of Middle-earth. It is in reality even darker, more perilous, and concerned primarily with the **intrigues of men**.

China Miéville and the backlash

In recent years, some writers (such as **China Miéville**—who cites his influences as H. P. Lovecraft, Mervyn Peake, and Michael Moorcock rather than Tolkien) have fought against the critical and commercial shadow that comes with the high fantasy label. Miéville has called Tolkien's influence "stultifying" and "pompous" and has **tried to switch the emphasis of his work** from a "Boy's Own" story glorying in war to a more picaresque take on fantasy adventure. Miéville's oeuvre has been influenced by many genres, from the western to noir. Despite his efforts, however, his narrative flourishes and attention to the landscape of his "subcreated" worlds is identifiably Tolkienesque. Miéville has now acknowledged Tolkien's influence and the inescapability of his work, **expressing admiration at the depth and scope of his achievements**.

3-Second Quest
The influence of Tolkien's creation goes much further than the popularity of wizards and hobbits. He showed new generations of writers in different genres how to create worlds.

Related Thoughts
see also
HIGH FANTASY
page 116
WIZARDS AND DRAGONS
page 120

❝ Middle-earth was not the first invented world, of course. But in the way the world is envisaged and managed, it represents a revolution. **❞**

CHINA MIÉVILLE

Terry Pratchett

China Miéville

Wizards and Dragons

Harry Potter

Perhaps the only stories to come near rivaling the worldwide successes of Tolkien's books are **J. K. Rowling's *Harry Potter*** novels. The debt to Tolkien is apparent in many ways, from the Nazgûl-esque threat of the Death-eaters, to giant spiders, Cave Trolls, magical emblems, and terrifying dark lords. But, like many modern writers, the influence of Tolkien is less a direct investment in the creative journey and more the inescapable nature of working in his wake. Rowling has cited a long list of influences, many of them overlapping with Tolkien's own. The *Harry Potter* books should be seen as another extremely successful sequence of stories that has found itself growing from the synthesis of the writer's own creative energies and influences including Tolkien and many others.

Teenage imaginations

One of the growth areas in the publishing industry has for many years centered on the market for **teenage fantasy fiction**. From the popular *Fighting Fantasy* role-play books first published by Puffin in the 1980s to Stephanie Meyer's *Twilight Saga*, the entire industry is largely indebted to the **astronomical success** of *The Lord of the Rings*. Some works of teenage fantasy fiction have close associations with Tolkien's works, such as Christopher Paolini's *Eragon*, while many others, from *Harry Potter* to *His Dark Materials*, exist in a market given impetus and shape by the commercial success of J. R. R. Tolkien.

Pulp Fiction

As Tolkien's US publishers saw the paperback sales of *The Lord of the Rings* shoot into the stratosphere during the 1960s, the industry began to see possibilities for tapping into the appetite (predominantly of teenage boys at first) for fantasy literature. This resulted in the beginnings of what was to become **an industry of paperback fantasy** as broad and as vast as Middle-earth itself. Many of the growing number of titles had highly alluring, colorful, and graphic cover art, often drawing heavily upon Tolkien's own illustrations and cartographic design work. The popularity of these books, which also took much inspiration from the sci-fi pulp fiction and **comics of the 40s and 50s**, helped change the entire landscape of teen publishing.

3-Second Quest
In the widest sense, the market for teenage fiction, as well as the market for all fantasy, has felt the influence of Tolkien's success.

Related Thoughts
see also
THE CHILDREN'S AUTHOR
page 50
HIGH FANTASY
page 116

❝*It was in fairy-stories that I first divined the potency of the words, and the wonder of things.*❞
ON FAIRY-STORIES

MYSTERY-ADVENTURE-ROMANCE

"THE MAGAZINE OF
PROPHETIC FICTION"

September

WONDER
Stories

25 CENTS
Canada 30¢

A GERNSBACK PUBLICATION

HUGO GERNSBACK Editor

Other Science Fiction Stories
By
FRANK J. BRIDGE

NATHAN SCHACHNER
and
ARTHUR L. ZAGAT

The Lord of the Rings Movies

Filming the unfilmable

The story of *The Lord of the Rings* straddles a perilous divide between cinematic and "unfilmable." The narrative, the adventure, the heroes and villains, and the excitement of the story all suggest that it **lends itself to cinema**; indeed, that it was made for it. But the sheer length of the story and the formidable depth of detail needed to create Middle-earth on screen has often seemed prohibitive. In the 1970s, **several animated versions** were made (a common treatment for perceived children's stories), the most poignant being the excellent but ill-fated **1978 Ralph Bakshi version**. Bakshi had planned to make the film in two parts, but after financiers pulled out the second film was never made.

An epic struggle

In an attempt to complete the story started by Bakshi (whose movie ends at the Battle of Helm's Deep), **Saul Zaentz**, the producer and owner of many of the Tolkien film and merchandise rights, encouraged the US television production company Rankin/Bass to make the sequel, *The Return of the King* **(1980)**. This version is much lighter, highly colorful, and aimed more directly at the children's market than Bakshi's dark vision. It also served as a sequel to Rankin/Bass's *The Hobbit*, which aired in the US in 1977. All the adaptations suffered from the need to truncate the epic into a **manageable storyline within limited budgets**.

A masterful interpretation

In 1997, New Zealand movie director **Peter Jackson**, who started out filming low-budget horror-comedies, met Saul Zaentz and negotiated for the rights to the movies. After much debate, and pressure from various studios who were concerned at the cost of making a trilogy rather than a single condensed version, **New Line Cinema** backed the venture and the filming of the trilogy began. Although Jackson was a successful director, and a popular one among horror fans, few could have predicted the success he would make of the adaptation. Indeed, his portfolio up to that point did not suggest that it would be Jackson who would direct **one of the most successful film franchises in history** and return Hollywood to the age of the epic blockbuster.

3-Second Quest
Tolkien's *The Lord of the Rings* came up against many problems in its long journey to the cinema screen; many of them due to the scope of the story.

Related Thoughts
see also
WINNING OSCARS
page 126
PETER JACKSON'S *THE HOBBIT*
page 128

" The film is a clash of a lot of styles like in all my films. I like moody backgrounds. I like drama. I like a lot of saturated color. **"**

RALPH BAKSHI

The Making of
The Lord of the Rings

Streamlining

For many, Peter Jackson's *The Lord of the Rings* trilogy is the movie epic to end all movie epics. Taking eight years to complete and with a reported budget of **$285 million**, Jackson not only fulfilled his vision but went as close as anyone is likely to in realizing the vision of Tolkien himself. Even a trilogy on this scale, however, involved the considerable task of **streamlining the structure**. Frodo's quest remains the central plotline, with Aragorn's story as the main subplot. Anything that did not tie in with either of these stories, such as the encounter with Tom Bombadil, was **cut from the script**.

The setting for Middle-earth

Jackon filmed the trilogy entirely in his native New Zealand, shooting all three movies consecutively in a little over a year. The **New Zealand landscape**, as diverse as it is breathtakingly beautiful, fitted extremely well with Jackson's vision of Middle-earth, which he has said was somewhere between Ray Harryhausen and David Lean. The production was an extremely tight affair, and a **family-like atmosphere** was common on set throughout. The cast members who made up the Fellowship famously got **matching tattoos** in a tattoo parlor in Wellington to commemorate the experience of making the movie. Each tattoo said "nine" in Tengwar—an elvish script created by Tolkien.

Using the technology

Jackson used and developed many of the **special effects techniques** that had been pioneered by the team working on Steven Spielberg's *Jurassic Park* in 1993. The trilogy contains just under **3,000 special effects shots**. Particularly inventive were the techniques used to portray the diminutive size of the hobbits, the motion-capture technology used to create an entirely CGI-represented character in Andy Serkis' Gollum, and, most impressively, the overall work that went into the awe-inspiring set piece at **the climax of *The Two Towers***—the Battle of Helm's Deep. Taking his cue from Spielberg's innovations, Jackson is now seen as the modern master of special effects.

3-Second Quest
Peter Jackson's *The Lord of the Rings* trilogy is seen by many as the epic to end all epics and has realized Tolkien's vision perfectly for millions of people.

Related Thoughts
see also
THE 'SEQUEL'
page 74
WINNING OSCARS
page 126

❝ What we were trying to do was to analyze what was important to Tolkien and to try to honor that. **❞**
PETER JACKSON

On set in
New Zealand

Winning Oscars

The anticipation

Peter Jackson's *The Lord of the Rings* trilogy was released in consecutive Decembers from **2001 to 2003** and was immediately a critical and commercial phenomenon. Indeed, even the trailer for the movie posted online in 2000 set a new record for download hits, notching up 1.7 million in the first 24 hours. The movies **broke many records** and threatened many more, becoming the biggest-grossing trilogy in cinema history (more even than *Star Wars*), and taking just under **$3 billion** worldwide. More often than not, the critical response was to be awestruck by the achievement of Jackson and his cast and crew.

From page to screen

The Lord of the Rings marks a truly remarkable moment in modern cinema. It is an epic in the classic sense, in the tradition of the director Cecil B. DeMille, but at the time of its release, it was also the **most technically innovative film** ever made. It saw one of the greatest works of literature of the twentieth century find its perfect assimilation into the visual medium, fulfilling the most demanding and vigorous needs of cinema. Although some of Tolkien's plotlines have changed, and Jackson's vision is **not a pure representation** of the story, for many the film realized the Middle-earth they had imagined from the time they first read the books. There can be few better examples than Jackson's trilogy of the potential of cinema to **bring literature to life**.

Award winners

Although *The Fellowship of the Ring* and *The Two Towers* did not perform particularly well at the **American Academy Awards**, *The Return of the King* equaled the previous record set by *Ben Hur* and *Titanic* by winning all **11 of the Oscars** for which it was nominated. Many people believe that the Academy voters had waited to honor the final movie as a nod to the trilogy as a whole. In total, *The Lord of the Rings* trilogy won **17 of its 30 nominations**. Perhaps the most demanding judges were the legions of faithful Tolkien readers, and although an eight-hour "fan edit" was released on DVD to modify the movies to the original storyline, most believe Jackson's original vision to be loyal to Tolkien.

3-Second Quest

Peter Jackson's trilogy became the highest-grossing filmic endeavor of all time, with cinema, DVD, and merchandise takings reportedly in the region of $8 billion.

Related Thoughts

see also
THE LORD OF THE RINGS MOVIES
page 122
THE MAKING OF
THE LORD OF THE RINGS
page 124

❝ [The Lord of the Rings] is an awesome production in its daring and breadth, and there are small touches that are just right.**❞**

ROGER EBERT,
CHICAGO SUN-TIMES,
2001

THE LORD OF THE RINGS
THE FELLOWSHIP OF THE RING

Peter Jackson's
The Hobbit

Bilbo's story

It was perhaps inevitable after the enormous success of *The Lord of the Rings* trilogy that Peter Jackson would be tempted to make a movie of *The Hobbit*. Surprisingly, Jackson announced that the story would be told over **three movies**: the first two released in consecutive Decembers in 2012 and 2013, with the final movie released in 2014. Many of the actors from *The Lord of the Rings* reprise their roles, with **Martin Freeman** taking the prized role of Bilbo Baggins. The release of *The Hobbit* is the culmination of a **unified vision for Tolkien's Middle-earth** on the big screen.

The journey to production

Jackson had originally voiced his desire to make *The Hobbit* in 1995, as part of a trilogy that would have seen the three books of *The Lord of the Rings* make up the second and third films. However, **complications over who owned the rights** for each book meant that Jackson directed *The Lord of the Rings* first. With many of the original complications disintegrating with time, Jackson at first decided to produce *The Hobbit* with maverick visionary and sci-fi director **Guillermo del Toro** taking the director's chair. Unfortunately, long legal wrangling and script delays meant that del Toro had scheduling conflicts and had to step down, although he retained a writer's credit. In 2010, Jackson was announced as director.

Darkening the tone

Jackson and del Toro had a healthy and creative working relationship, and many decisions made by del Toro during his time at the helm were upheld by Jackson. One **important concept** was to make the tone of *The Hobbit* something closer to *The Lord of the Rings* trilogy. Del Toro has spoken of the need to begin *The Hobbit* with a light and somewhat naïve feel with the playful companionship of the Dwarves, before **leading the viewer to a darker place**—a world of corruption and greed. He has likened the mood to that of the coming of the First World War—a shadow growing over the relaxed and **ostentatious garden parties** of Europe in the earliest days of the twentieth century.

3-Second Quest

It may have been inevitable that Peter Jackson would go on to direct *The Hobbit*, but his greatest challenge was to unify the tone of this movie and his previous trilogy.

Related Thoughts

see also
THE HOBBIT
page 66
THE MAKING OF *THE HOBBIT*
page 130

❝I think The Hobbit is a bit more colorful. And a bit more operatic. And whimsical. One of the things the book marks very strongly is the seasons, so we're using that as the basis of our thought.**❞**

GUILLERMO DEL TORO

Guillermo del Toro

Martin Freeman
as Bilbo Baggins

The Making of *The Hobbit*

Cutting-edge technology

Peter Jackson controversially announced that he would shoot his movies at **48 frames per second** rather than the usual 24. Purists felt this represented a move away from the grainy feel of true cinema. Jackson, who also shot the movies in 3-D, always works at the cutting edge of cinema technology. He went to great pains to assure moviegoers that his filming would create a **new kind of realism** for lovers of fantasy and prove to be the future of moviemaking. The audience's first reaction to samples was less than euphoric, but **Peter Jackson stood by his innovation**. One thing is for certain: the technology used on *The Hobbit* is essential to creating a trilogy to rival the wonder of *The Lord of the Rings*.

Two becomes three

Once again, Jackson filmed the movie in **New Zealand**, often at undisclosed locations. Many of the sites used in *The Hobbit* will be familiar to those who know *The Lord of the Rings* movies, with sets being reprised. Perhaps the most complicated piece of this **moviemaking puzzle** was the structure of the story. At first *The Hobbit* had been a two-movie project. Guillermo del Toro had his own ideas of where to split the story, such as after Smaug's death, but Jackson had some choices to make of his own. Eventually, with such a wealth of material, Jackson realized that he had another trilogy on his hands. In July 2012 the director confirmed **a three-movie structure** for *The Hobbit*.

Jackson's interpretation

Using a combination of creative license and the source of **Tolkien's vast Middle-earth history** that exists extraneous to the adventures of the hobbits, Jackson has given certain elements of the book more substance. Gandalf's own adventures, for instance, the period when he is away consulting the White Council and his confrontation with the **Necromancer**, are given full screentime, also serving up opportunities for these films to interweave solidly with the *The Lord of the Rings* movies. Also, many characters from *The Lord of the Rings* who do not appear in the book are given plot strands in *The Hobbit*, thus helping to **tie the narrative tightly** to Frodo's subsequent adventure. As with Tolkien's writing, Peter Jackson's movie-making has developed a living, growing, and interweaving mythology.

3-Second Quest
In many ways, *The Hobbit* movies reflect more of Jackson's influence than *The Lord of the Rings*, with many plot strands and characters devised by Jackson himself.

Related Thoughts
see also
THE HOBBIT
page 66
PETER JACKSON'S *THE HOBBIT*
page 128

"I want it to seem like we've gone back on location into Middle-earth; that these... movies feel like they belong at the beginning of the other three. We're the same filmmakers going into the same world.**"**

PETER JACKSON

On set in Bilbo's hobbit hole

Gandalf deep in thought

Tolkien's Influence on Movies

Quest movies

One of the most significant trends to come from the global success of *The Lord of the Rings* books was the turning of marketing departments in publishers and movie studios to the new appetite for fantastical adventure. At first, Tolkien's influence was not entirely obvious, as none of his stories were being produced in **Hollywood**. But the studios were plundering established myths of the ancient world with the *Sinbad* series (1958–77), *Jason and the Argonauts* (1963), and *Clash of the Titans* (1981). The mixture of the **heroic quest**, the world familiar to us but darkened by the perilous mischief of magical beings, and the **band-of-brothers adventure**, was central to Tolkien's work, and this began to flavor Hollywood's idea of adventure.

Star Wars

As much as it is difficult to imagine modern cinema without the shadow of George Lucas's *Star Wars* franchise, it is equally difficult to imagine **Star Wars** without the influence of Tolkien. At its core, *Star Wars* is the story of a young and naive character who becomes caught up in a conflict that has ramifications far beyond his humble world, a conflict that could end the Universe. Luke Skywalker is assisted by a **curious group of adventurers**, not least an old man with a beard and mystical powers whose origins are shrouded in the mystery of a quasi-religious order. The young protagonist has to find an integral strength that he did not know he had in order to defeat a **colossal dark power**.

A fellowship of fantasy

As a direct result of the phenomenal success of *Star Wars*, very much "*The Lord of the Rings* in space," fantasy became one of the **most popular genres** in Hollywood. By the 1980s, movies such as *Krull*, *Willow*, *Labyrinth*, and *Jabberwocky* followed a trend that would lead ultimately to Peter Jackson's Tolkien movies in the 2000s. Along the way, **the superhero movie** was in turn deeply influenced by Jackson's technical innovations. Away from Hollywood, Tolkien's vision of fantasy also laid heavy feet. **Studio Ghibli**, Japan's most successful animation studio, and maker of some of the most enchanting fantasy movies of the last 30 years, began life as Topcraft, the company responsible for much of the animation in the 1977 Rankin/Bass version of *The Hobbit*.

3-Second Quest
Tolkien's influence is felt deep and wide in cinema, from quest movies to space operas, to 80s B-movies, to Japan's most wonderful anime.

Related Thoughts
see also
AFTER TOLKIEN
page 104
THE LORD OF THE RINGS
MOVIES
page 122

❝ You've got to compete head on with these other epic works of fantasy and fiction, the Tolkiens and the 'Star Wars'... People want a persistent alternate reality to invest themselves in... that makes it rich and worth their time. **❞**

JAMES CAMERON

Studio Ghibli, animators of the early Tolkien adaptations

Music

The instrumental landscape

Great works of literature have always inspired other forms of art, not least music. It is no surprise that the vivid descriptions of the vast sweeping landscapes of Middle-earth have inspired celebrated pieces of **orchestral music** such as the fabulous award-winning scores for the Peter Jackson movies by Howard Shore. Composers such as Aulis Sallinen, Ensio Kosta, and Paul Corfield Godfrey have created music based on the characters of Tolkien's stories to great effect. Also, with the **Saul Zaentz-produced musical** of *The Lord of the Rings* transferring from Toronto to London in 2007, composers A. R. Rahman and Christopher Nightingale found their work nominated for **Olivier Awards**. Some musicians have put music to Tolkien's folk songs, most successfully Donald Swann, whose work met with Tolkien's own approval.

Led Zeppelin

One of the most notable uses of Tolkien's work in popular music was by fans Jimmy Page and Robert Plant of **Led Zeppelin**, who wrote many hugely successful songs referencing the mythology and landscape of Middle-earth. On their second album, *Led Zeppelin II*, the song "Ramble On" refers directly to Mordor and a **magical ring**. Page and Plant were from a folk and blues background, so their use of Tolkien's mythopoeia as inspiration is no surprise. The rock gods of the late 1960s and '70s drew on the symbolism of **Olympian mysticism**, and it was a natural progression to be drawn into Tolkien's universe. By the mid-70s there was a defined link between Tolkien's work and the progressive rock movement—not always a flattering one as bands progressed from epic to epically self-indulgent.

Heavy metal

In part due to the works of Led Zeppelin, the granddaddies of **heavy metal**, this music genre has felt the influence of Tolkien's work most potently. Many musicians have been attracted by the **inventiveness of Tolkien's languages**, with groups mining his work for band names such as Cirith Ungol, Isengard, and Amon Amarth. The influence of Tolkien even breaks through the corrugated distortion of metal's walls of power chords and seems to soften the sound of the music itself, which incorporates folksy, **Anglo-Saxon undertones** in the work not only of Zeppelin but of Austrian band Summoning, and the dark, prickly music of Gorgoroth.

3-Second Quest
Tolkien's influence on musicians has been varied but constant, from classical composers to the darkest corners of progressive rock and heavy metal.

Related Thoughts
see also
TOLKIEN'S INFLUENCE ON MOVIES
page 132
FANTASY ART
page 134

" *The cycles should be linked to a majestic whole, and yet leave scope for other minds and hands, wielding paint and music and drama.* **"**
THE LETTERS OF J.R.R. TOLKIEN

The Lord of the Rings
with live orchestration

THE
LORD OF THE RINGS
THE FELLOWSHIP OF THE RING

Jimmy Page of
Led Zeppelin

Fantasy Art

Earthly delights

Fantasy art can trace its origins as far back as the myth and magic of ancient cultures, and is often linked to religious expression—notably in the Hieronymus Bosch work of 1500, *The Garden of Earthly Delights*. Tolkien's work unleashed a modern age of fantasy artists, both in the few illustrating his writing directly and the many inspired by it. Tolkien's own artwork was used, witness the evocative mountains of the original cover for *The Hobbit*, while **Pauline Baynes** and **Queen Margrethe II of Denmark** were admired collaborators. As Middle-earth began to inspire role-playing games, calendars, and collectibles, highly respected illustrators such as **Angus McBride** and the Hugo-award-winning American **Tim Kirk** rose to the challenge of depicting the wonders and characters of Tolkien's world.

Middle-earth artists

What Tolkien's work offered artists was the invaluable facility for unbridled imagination, through his striking landscapes, **unique characters**, and dark perils. He helped rejuvenate an artistic interest in fantastical creatures and heroic notions that had perhaps lain dormant since the Pre-Raphaelites. Peter Jackson drew upon the modern generation of fantasy painters for the visual dynamics of his movies, bringing in much-admired Tolkien artists **John Howe and Alan Lee** to advise him. Both artists have a huge fanbase stemming from their work on Tolkien-related projects that date back to the 1990s, including book cover designs and calendar art. Jackson brought them in to "authenticate" the feel of the movies, Howe even taking the lead on **designing the weaponry** and armor for the characters.

A broader landscape

As Tolkien's vision became infused into a fantasy industry that was soon to incorporate all aspects of entertainment, including **video games**, board games, cinema, and theater, his dramatic landscapes and iconic characters and creatures became a standard for artists. Giants of twentieth-century fantasy art such as **Frank Frazetta** (whose classic Death Dealer paintings are certainly channeled into the form of Bakshi's Nazgûl in his 1977 *The Lord of the Rings* movie) and later contemporary artists such as Bob Eggleton and Michael Whelan clearly draw influence from the Tolkien canon. With Whelan in particular, it is striking how the enormous vistas of the **fantastical backdrops** of his subcreated worlds are almost precursors to the New Zealand settings of Peter Jackson's movies.

3-Second Quest
The influence of Tolkien on fantasy art ended up feeding directly and organically into Peter Jackson's vision for his movie adaptations.

Related Thoughts
see also
MUSIC
page 134
ROLE-PLAYING COMPUTER GAMES
page 134

❝I had read The Lord of the Rings when I was about 17... I just loved the whole world that he created and so it was a dream come true really to get the chance to illustrate the books later on.**❞**
ALAN LEE

*The Garden of
Earthly Delights*
by Hieronymus Bosch

Angus McBride's
working drawings for
Ent, Orc, and Gollum

Fans and Conventions

The Tolkien Society

In 1968 the UK Tolkien Society, which has become the headquarters for Tolkien fans and societies, was established. It publishes a magazine and runs annual conventions. In the US, the Tolkien Society of America was absorbed into the **Mythopoeic Society**, which still runs today, assimilating fandom with academic ambition in the study of Tolkien's work. The fans, in addition to studying in minute detail the work of the great man, have a reputation for **dressing up** as their favorite Middle-earth characters. Hobbits, Wizards, Orcs, and Men of Gondor are common sights at yearly fantasy conventions, such as **Comic-Con in San Diego**, Mythcon (the Mythopoeic Society conference), and Oxonmoot (the Tolkien Society gathering, which takes place in Oxford on or near September 22—the birthday of Frodo and Bilbo Baggins).

Tolkien in translation

It is not just in the US and the UK that fans have formed Tolkien Societies. Scandinavia, responding to Tolkien's love and admiration for its historic Old Norse sagas, has many spin-off organizations, including the Tolkien Society Forodrim. Greece has a Tolkien fanclub called **The Prancing Pony**, named after the inn where the hobbits meet Aragorn for the first time, and Japan has The White Rider, a fanclub that was formed after the movies were released. Tolkien fanclubs now gather online and off all over the world, in every conceivable country, from Israel to Peru, with regular meetings and parties as well as **vibrant online forums** for discussions about all things Middle-earth.

The homages

In 2009, Independent Online Cinema released one of the most accomplished homages in all of fandom in the form of *The Hunt for Gollum*, a **full-length feature movie** filmed by fans of Tolkien and Jackson's films. It is a remarkably assured piece of moviemaking with superb attention to detail and production values, and in some places aspires to the scope and ambition of Jackson. But **The Hunt for Gollum** is just the finest example of the lengths to which fans of *The Lord of the Rings* will go to celebrate their heroes. To see preview footage of Jackson's *The Hobbit*, fans camped for several days at 2012's Comic-Con. Many fans have even dedicated themselves to becoming **fluent in Tolkien's languages**.

3-Second Quest
Tolkien fans have become renowned worldwide as some of the most dedicated in any cultural area.

Related Thoughts
see also
ENDURING POPULARITY
page 112
WINNING OSCARS
page 126

[on his US fans]
" Art moves them and they don't know what they've been moved by and they get quite drunk on it. Many young Americans are involved in the stories in a way that I'm not. **"**

J.R.R. TOLKIEN: A BIOGRAPHY

INDEPENDENT ONLINE CINEMA
PRESENTS

THE HUNT FOR GOLLUM

A FILM INSPIRED BY
THE LORD OF THE RINGS

NOT ALL WHO WANDER ARE LOST.

3RD MAY 2009

THE HUNT FOR GOLLUM

NOT ALL WHO WANDER ARE LOST

THE HUNT BEGINS MAY 3RD 2009

Role-Playing Fantasy Games

The launch of new realms

Around the time of Tolkien's death in 1973, the company Tactical Studies Rules was preparing to launch its board game, **Dungeons & Dragons**. The company directors and the game's designers, Dave Arneson and Gary Gygax, openly acknowledged two main influences for the game's world, creatures, and magic: the *Conan* books of **Robert E. Howard** and the Middle-earth works of J. R. R. Tolkien. In the original Dungeons & Dragons, many creatures were taken directly from Tolkien's work, such as hobbits, Elves, Dwarfs, Nazgûl, and Orcs, as well as Men and Wizards. Later, these were replaced by more generic terms, such as halfling for hobbit and specter for Nazgûl; Orcs reverted to goblin and Balrogs became the rather more technically named Type IV Demon.

The gaming experience

Dungeons & Dragons spawned not only myriad imitators but a new section of the entertainment industry—the **fantasy role-playing** game. Dungeons & Dragons was a revolutionary, totally immersive fantasy experience for fans of the literature, and it became a global sensation. The players could assume the role of any character from the Tolkien universe, from Dwarf fighter to halfling thief, and would spend nights (or even days or months) working their way through the scenarios created by their **Dungeon Master**. The game created a whole new world for children (and many adults) seeking imaginative and unrelenting escapist adventure. Today, the "offspring" of Dungeons & Dragons have created an entirely new social strata of "**fantasy gamers**."

MERP

MERP (Middle-earth Role Playing) was a dice game that made its appearance with the guidebook of 1984. **MERP** was played through prewritten scenarios with two 10-sided dice, each player having sets of attributes to fight the enemy. The game was not based upon **Tolkien's stories** but rather took place in his world (sometimes in the most obscure and barely explored parts of Middle-earth), giving the gamewriters free reign to create what they liked for the drama of the moment. Although popular, MERP was not for the fainthearted. With a **complex rule system** and potential for a bewildering mixture of potentialities, the players needed to draw on extensive knowledge of Tolkien's mythopoeia as well as histories written by the gamewriters themselves.

3-Second Quest
In many ways, with the invention of fantasy role-playing games, Tolkien was a major instigator of an entirely new strand of the entertainment industry.

Related Thoughts
see also
FANS AND CONVENTIONS
page 138
ROLE-PLAYING COMPUTER GAMES
page 142

❝ *Indeed, who can doubt the excellence of Tolkien's writing? So of course it had a strong impact on A/D&D [Advanced Dungeons & Dragons] games.* **❞**
GARY GYGAX

**Many-sided dice,
for role-playing games**

Fantasy role-playing figures

GELDER

Role-Playing Computer Games

Early examples

In 1982, with the cooperation of Tolkien's publishers, game developers Beam Software released one of the most popular games of the **early days of computers**—The Hobbit. The game was an innovative adventure and role-play experience using the parser technology specifically designed to make it as realistic an experience as was on offer at the time, allowing the player to talk to the characters onscreen. By the end of the 1980s, the game had sold more than a million copies, won a **Golden Joystick Award** for best strategy game, and spawned several Tolkien-based sequels that incorporated the story of *The Lord of the Rings*. Each game came with a copy of the book that had inspired it.

Warhammer

One of the most significant gaming phenomena in the field of fantasy in the last 30 years was the establishment of **Games Workshop** and **Warhammer** in the 1970s. For many years, Warhammer (the brainchild of fantasy impresarios Steve Jackson and Ian Livingstone) concentrated on board games and dice books. But in 1991 it made the first foray into the world of computer games with **Hero Quest**—an adaptation of a **role-playing board game** from MB. It was around this time that software manufacturers began to see the potential for fantasy games from both a gameplay and a design point of view; and game designers, whether they were aware of it or not, were never far from Tolkien's influence.

Into the modern world

The technology and design nous of today's computer games have changed the nature of gaming entirely, and the fantasy genre dominates the market. With the innovations of **3-D graphics**, game developers and designers soon had an armory that could potentially match Tolkien's imagination. Most notable of the games to evolve from Tolkien's influence are the Zelda series (a quest and role-play game that added playable action to the puzzle-solving of Beam Software's The Hobbit), and the series **The Elder Scrolls**, which has closer ties to Tolkien with its characters including Wood-elves and Dwarves. The latest incarnation of these role-players, in addition to those EA and **Warner Brothers** have published to tie in with Peter Jackson's movies, are a far cry from Beam's humble beginnings.

3-Second Quest
Computer games would look very different today had it not been for the early influence of fantasy and quest narratives, both of which owe enormous debts to Tolkien.

Related Thoughts
see also
ROLE-PLAYING FANTASY GAMES
page 140
OTHER WORLDS
page 144

❝ *[The] instruction to us was, 'Write the best Adventure game ever.' So Philip [Mitchell] and I designed and wrote The Hobbit.* **❞**
VERONIKA MEGLER,
GAME DESIGNER

Other Worlds

Virtual worlds

Along with **innovations in game development** in the field of online gaming, fantasy adventures have become a part of a much larger picture. It is difficult to imagine how the industry that is now made up of virtual worlds online could exist without the figure of Tolkien foreshadowing so much of it. A brief glimpse into the landscapes of, for example, **World of Warcraft** (a game that claims more than 10 million participants worldwide), is a glimpse into the strength and power of the influence of **Tolkien's imagination** over everything that has come since. Players can control figures that trace their lineage to Tolkien's oeuvre, and manipulate those figures through a decidedly Tolkienesque world.

Influence of computer games

If **a virtual environment**, created on an international computer network, was the last place Tolkien might have imagined his vision, then he would have perhaps cast a wry smile at the direction the story takes next. As the commercial industry of **gaming overtakes every other aspect** of the entertainment universe, so the games that have derived from Tolkien's imagination have begun to filter back into literature and movies. Hollywood spends hundreds of millions of dollars every year creating narrative-driven scripts based on computer games, from the **Resident Evil** franchise to **Assassin's Creed**. Collaborative creatives, such as writer R. A. Salvatore, are converging on the world of gaming to create entire mythopoeia, seeing it as the future of the entertainment industry.

Tolkien in space

While the growing number of virtual worlds have provided ideal settings for Tolkien's mythology to expand and evolve, his influence can also be seen in the reality of our own Solar System. Given the popular association between "geek" **scientists and high fantasy**, it is perhaps not surprising that the Tolkien name has soared with a big bang into astronomical nomenclature. An asteroid discovered in 1982, which orbits between Jupiter and Mars, was named **2675 Tolkien** in the author's honor, along with the asteroid 2991 Bilbo. In 2012, NASA's scientists discovered a series of craters near Mercury's north pole by the Messenger (Mercury Surface, Space Environment, Geochemistry and Ranging) probe. On the Mordor-like surface, keeping company with Kandinsky and Prokofiev there is now the **Tolkien crater**.

3-Second Quest
Without Tolkien, the world of online gaming would be very different. He gave us its characters, its towns, forests, and mountain ranges, and he gave it the seeds of infinite adventures.

Related Thoughts
see also
ROLE-PLAYING COMPUTER GAMES
page 142
CONSERVATION AND LANDSCAPE
page 148

❝Tolkien reminded me of some dear elements I had lost: the joy of reading; the pleasure of the imagination; the love of adventure. It all came back to me.❞
R. A. SALVATORE

Gryphon Rider, 2003,
by Bill Petras for
World of Warcraft

The northern pole of
Mercury, where the
Tolkien Crater is located

Language

Coining words

As with most great writers and cultural phenomena, from Shakespeare to J. K. Rowling, many of the **phrases and words** that Tolkien coined have passed into common usage in the English language. Tolkien's profession as a philologist and his role as a lexicographer with the *Oxford English Dictionary* meant that he spent much of his time in the fascinating labyrinths of word games and **etymological spirals**. This fed into his own **created languages**, of course, but it also informed his use of English as he chose words with resonances that are not immediately obvious to most readers. Words such as "mannish," "dwarvish" or "dwarven," "halfling," and "bane" all owe something of their popular use, if not their origins, to Tolkien.

The obsolete

"Confusticate," "blunderbuss," and "corrigan" are just three obsolete words that Tolkien uses in **important moments** of his work. Tolkien enjoyed digging deep into language and often throwing these odd, jarring, playful words into the mouths of his characters. They can be extremely effective and influential, and it was with good reason that he reclaimed such musical words as "**dumbledoor**," a dialectical name for the bumblebee which went on to influence J. K. Rowling in the naming of one of her most popular characters. There are less famous, but just as striking, examples. When Éowyn strikes down the Witch-king in *The Return of the King,* she calls him a "**foul dwimmerlaik**," a word of complex origin, derivatives of which have been used in *Dungeons & Dragons* and fantasy literature.

Period prose

Today, "period prose" is a recognized trait of both fantasy and historical literature. Although it was used to great effect by a few popular writers, such as **Sir Walter Scott** in his nationalist epics and medieval adventures, Tolkien combined the use of period prose with his **Middle-earth languages** and affected archaisms to help create an atmosphere and an otherworldliness that did not interfere with the telling of the story but gave it an authentic quality. The prose that Tolkien used to such great effect was a mixture of contemporary English and a **pseudo-medieval tongue**. This would have been, for a man of such scholarship in this area, a conscious decision—both to emulate the great myths he admired and to heighten the language and its connection with his audience.

3-Second Quest
Tolkien's philological approach to names and his proud archaic prose styles have influenced generations of fantasy writers and molded the sound and look of entire worlds to come in literature, movies, and gaming.

Related Thoughts
see also
TEACHER AND SCHOLAR
page 40
MYTHOLOGY
page 90

❝ *Tolkien often comments on how the contemplation of an individual word can be the starting point for an adventure in imagination.* ❞

GILLIVER, MARSHALL, AND WEINER, *THE RING OF WORDS*

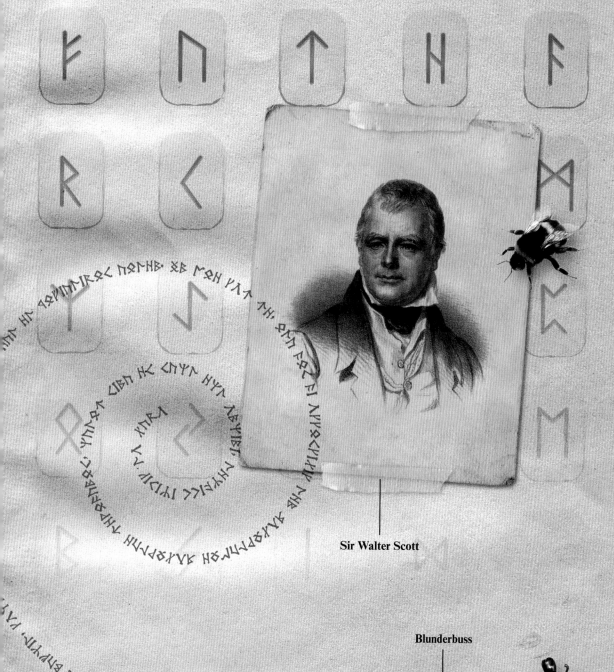

Sir Walter Scott

Blunderbuss

Conservation and Landscape

The modernist

In literary terms, Tolkien could be said to be a modernist. His concerns with the impending threat over the countryside he so loved, the England by which he defined himself, is a powerful theme in the writings of other authors who were uncomfortably labeled with the term "modernism," such as **Edward Thomas**, **Robert Frost**, and **W. B. Yeats**. Most writers of Tolkien's generation were greatly affected by the grim experiences of war and were left with an apocalyptic sense of the oncoming of the dark, industrial colors to the lights of the **English country garden**. Tolkien's vision was one of victory over these powers and has been held up as such ever since in literary, political, and environmental movements that take energy from the popularity and optimism of his work.

A countryside champion

Tolkien has become a figurehead not just for many environmentalists but, more specifically, for those fighting for a certain type of landscape. His concerns were primarily for the "Oxford" type of greenery and English spring; crudely put, he idealized nature in the form of the Shire. All around the world today conservation schemes and country and mountain walks, such as the **Tolkien Trail** in Lancashire, UK, which are subject to protective schemes, bear his name almost as a good-luck charm for the fortunes of the area. In the wake of the Peter Jackson movies, the **New Zealand Department of Conservation** has seen a spectacular flourishing in its tourist activity; which, in turn, provides help and promotion for environmental work across the national landscape.

A moral legacy

What Tolkien achieved with his work was to provide a basis for readers to approach the subject now known as "**environmentalism**" from a merging of neo-pagan and Christian belief systems. The morality underpinning Middle-earth is not just Judeo-Christian it is specifically Catholic, although none of this is overt in his writing. The ethos of Middle-earth is one without an Old Testament God, and one without Jesus Christ. Tolkien strips away the need for such premises and allows the reader to connect with the essence of nature and to respect the precariousness of **the natural world** in the face of the gray and impersonal soullessness of modernity.

3-Second Quest
Tolkien has been rightly identified as one of the twentieth century's most important and passionate environmentalist writers.

Related Thoughts
see also
OXFORD
page 30
MIDDLE-EARTH
page 94

❝ *The putting together of various elements to shape an ecologically deep environmental vision is one of the things that J. R. R. Tolkien accomplished supremely well more than half a century ago.* **❞**
DICKERSON, EVANS,
ENTS, ELVES, AND ERIADOR

W. B. Yeats

Hobbiton,
New Zealand

Legacy of Life and Works

The intellectual world

J. R. R. Tolkien's influence upon modern popular culture is so vast, is so deep, that in some places it goes unnoticed, and in others it seems a **generic cliché**. In the world of fantasy, for example, barely a shred of substance has not felt his touch in some aspect. Tolkien re-created fantasy, and in the process changed not only how writers viewed the ways in which they could approach their subjects but forged an **entertainment industry** that knows no bounds. As other writers stretched intellectual boundaries, it was Tolkien who suggested that the inner world could be a place to build outer worlds also. From board games to **epic cinema**, from unlikely heroes to entire races of people, Tolkien has played a significant part in how the modern intellectual world was created.

The work of the man

For all of Tolkien's creations, he was a man born of his own experiences and passions. What Tolkien invested into his "**subcreations**" were exactly the idiosyncrasies that went into making him who he was. Through his desire to entertain his young children, he composed his life's opus. Indeed, he put his life into the world of **heroes and villains** and from there reflected upon generations of readers in ways that a mere moralizing essayist or philosopher could never do. It is in this purity of intent and goodness of spirit that Tolkien perhaps makes himself best known. For example, as each reader reacts to the fortitude of Frodo, they are reacting to the fortitude of those who died in the **First World War**; as they react to the strength of the Fellowship, they are reacting to every friend they have ever had.

A moral legacy

Tolkien may have spawned a thousand imitators, but his greatest legacy is perhaps the possibilities that he opened up for the **creative minds** that came after him. From Alan Garner to Peter Jackson, from C. S. Lewis to J. K. Rowling, Tolkien has given the world the opportunity to experience the creative energies of an entirely new breed of **visionary**. In so doing, he has created possibilities for the highbrow and lowbrow alike, as no other has done before. No writer has seen his work branch off into such diverse areas—from the online gaming of **World of Warcraft** to the dystopic visions of Doris Lessing. It is perhaps this depth of influence that makes Tolkien one of the truly great literary figures.

3-Second Quest
Tolkien's gift came from his own beliefs and his own good nature. It has resulted in a very rare influence upon all strands of our intellectual and popular universe.

Related Thoughts
see also
SUCCESS
page 56
THE ACADEMIC
page 102

❝I do not love the bright sword for its sharpness, nor the arrow for its swiftness, nor the warrior for his glory. I love only that which they defend.**❞**

FARAMIR, *THE TWO TOWERS*

Timeline

1950-56
The publication of the seven volumes of C. S. Lewis's *The Chronicles of Narnia*.

1957
The Lord of the Rings wins the International Fantasy Award at the 15th World Science Fiction Convention.

1957
Alan Garner's first novel, *The Weirdstone of Brisingamen*, is published.

1961
Tolkien is nominated for the Nobel Prize by C. S. Lewis. He loses out to Ivo Andric.

1968
The UK Tolkien Society is founded.

1969
Led Zeppelin release their first album and record several songs influenced by Tolkien's creations over the next decade.

1973
Frank Frazetta's first *Death Dealer* painting goes on display.

1974
Dungeons & Dragons goes on the market.

1976
John Howe discovers the artwork of the Hildebrandt brothers' calendar of Middle-earth and immediately begins drawing.

1977
Ralph Bakshi's animated movie *The Lord of the Rings* is released as Part one of the story. Part two was never to be made.

1982
Beam software releases the groundbreaking role-playing computer game The Hobbit.

1984
The first MERP book comes on the market.

1987
John Howe's first Tolkien calendar is released.

1991
Warhammer makes its first foray into fantasy video games with Hero Quest.

1994
The first of the series of The Elder Scrolls video games is released.

1996
Game of Thrones, the first in George R.R. Martin's *Song of Ice and Fire* series of high fantasy novels is released.

1997
Harry Potter and the Philosopher's Stone is published, the first of seven books by J. K. Rowling that go on to sell over 450 million copies worldwide.

2001
Peter Jackson releases *The Fellowship of the Ring*, the first of his movie adaptations of *The Lord of the Rings*.

2004
The Lord of the Rings comes top in the BBC poll of the nation's favorite books.

2004
The Return of the King movie wins all 11 of the Oscars for which it was nominated, equaling the previous record of wins.

2006
The Saul Zaentz-produced stage musical begins its life in Toronto, Canada.

2009
The fan feature movie *The Hunt for Gollum* is released online.

2012–14
Peter Jackson releases his three-part adaptations of *The Hobbit*.

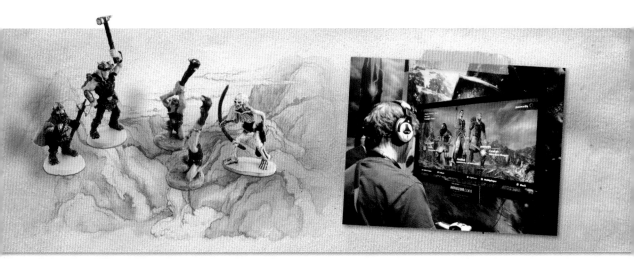

Glossary

Ralph Bakshi An American director who created an animated movie of *The Lord of the Rings*, produced by Saul Zaentz, in 1978, but ran out of funding to complete the filming of the second movie.

Pauline Baynes An English book illustrator favored by Tolkien for her interpretations of his work.

Dungeons & Dragons A role-playing board game launched in 1973 that became a worldwide success. Tolkien's world was one of its main sources.

High fantasy A genre created by Tolkien in which a story is set in an alternative world.

Peter Jackson The New Zealand director of *The Lord of the Rings* and *The Hobbit* trilogies known for his use of innovative technologies.

MERP (Middle-earth Role-Playing)
A role-playing dice game launched in 1984 in which stories took place in the world of Middle-earth.

Mythopoeic Society The US Tolkien fanbase that incorporates the Tolkien Society of America.

Period prose Archaic language used in a narrative to create a certain atmosphere within the text.

Rankin/Bass An American production company that produced an animated movie of *The Hobbit* in 1977 and *The Return of the King* in 1980.

Role-playing A game in which players assume roles of fantasy characters with attributes determined by dice and a rule book. The players are guided through story scenarios by a Dungeon Master.

Subcreation Tolkien's word describing the creation of an alternative world in which to set a story.

Donald Swann A British composer who set Tolkien's poems from *The Lord of the Rings* to song in a volume called *The Road Goes Ever On*.

Tolkien Society The headquarters of Tolkien fanclubs worldwide, based in the UK.

Virtual worlds Online communities in which people have characters, called avatars, who can interact with each other in a created 3-D world.

Warhammer Distributed by Games Workshop, the Warhammer series of games are popular role-play scenarios that grew into a computer game in the early 1990s.

Saul Zaentz An American movie producer who owns the movie, stage, and merchandise rights to *The Hobbit* and *The Lord of the Rings*. He produced Bakshi's 1978 movie.

3-Minute Summary

Life

John Ronald Reuel Tolkien was born on **January 3, 1892**, in Bloemfontein, South Africa. An orphan at age 12, Tolkien remained a devout Roman Catholic, becoming a loving father, husband, and valued friend. King Edward's School cultivated his academic promise and linguistic propensity, and he went on to **study at Oxford**. Tolkien **fought at the Battle of the Somme**, where he lost some of his dearest friends. After the war and a period of teaching in Leeds, he became a professor at Oxford and spent 30 years as a dynamic member of the English faculty at Pembroke College. By the time of his **death in 1973**, Tolkien was world famous for his fantasy stories and was also a legendary presence of Oxford academe.

Work

From childhood, Tolkien enjoyed creating languages, drawing on his studies of European and Scandinavian **medieval cultures**. These languages eventually gave birth to new races of beings, and by early adulthood Tolkien was creating his own **mythopoeia**—a creative process that would last the rest of his life. Much of this would be included in his life's work, *The Silmarillion*, and go on to form the basis for his greatest **adventure stories**, *The Hobbit* and *The Lord of the Rings*. His creations helped reinvent the fantasy genre, and figures such as Bilbo Baggins, Gandalf, and Smaug the Magnificent have become **iconic**. He also wrote many smaller fantastical tales and contributed groundbreaking academic papers during a career that changed the way Old English texts were studied.

Influence

Few writers have had such an influence on popular culture as J. R. R. Tolkien. You can find his fingerprints on the farthest reaches of the **entertainment industry**, from the song lyrics of Led Zeppelin to the landscapes of popular online virtual worlds. Peter Jackson's **cinematic adaptation** of *The Lord of the Rings* has become the most critically and commercially successful film trilogy of all time, spawning not only limitless imitations of its technical innovations but also leading to his version of *The Hobbit*. Tolkien's imagination has been a major influence on **environmentalism and philology**. As for his readers, he has been the focus of intense fan worship across the globe, and he frequently tops national public polls of favorite writers.

> **"**I desired dragons with a profound desire. Of course, I in my timid body did not wish to have them in the neighborhood, intruding into my relatively safe world, in which it was, for instance, possible to read stories in peace of mind, free from fear. But the world that contained even the imagination of Fáfnir was richer and more beautiful, at whatever cost of peril.**"**
>
> *ON FAIRY-STORIES*

Resources

Books

The Hobbit
J. R. R. Tolkien
HOUGHTON MIFFLIN BOOKS FOR CHILDREN, 2012

The Legend of Sigurd and Gudrun
J. R. R. Tolkien, Christopher Tolkien
HOUGHTON MIFFLIN HARCOURT, 2009

The Lord of the Rings
J. R. R. Tolkien
MARINER BOOKS, 2012

The Monsters and the Critics and Other Essays
J. R. R. Tolkien
GRAFTON, 1997

On Fairy-stories
J. R. R. Tolkien
HARPERCOLLINS, 2008

The Silmarillion
J. R. R. Tolkien, Christopher Tolkien, Ted Naismith
HOUGHTON MIFFLIN HARCOURT, 2004

Tales from the Perilous Realm
J. R. R. Tolkien, illustrated by Alan Lee
HOUGHTON MIFFLIN HARCOURT, 2008

Sources

The Art of the Hobbit
J. R. R. Tolkien
HOUGHTON MIFFLIN HARCOURT, 2012

The Atlas of Middle-earth
Karen Wynn Fonstad
MARINER BOOKS, 2001

Ents, Elves, and Eriador
Matthew Dickerson, Jonathan Evans
UNIVERSITY PRESS OF KENTUCKY, 2011

J. R. R. Tolkien, A Biography
Humphrey Carpenter and J. R. R. Tolkien
HOUGHTON MIFFLIN COMPANY, 2000

J. R. R. Tolkien, Author of the Century
Tom Shippey
MARINER BOOKS, 2002

The J. R. R. Tolkien Companion
Christina Scull, Wayne G. Hammond
HOUGHTON, MIFFLIN HARCOURT, 2006

Languages, Myths and History
Elizabeth Solopova
NORTH LANDING BOOKS, 2009

The Letters of J. R. R. Tolkien
J. R. R. Tolkien, Christopher Tolkien, Humphrey Carpenter
MARINER BOOKS, 2000

The Lord of the Rings Sketchbook
Alan Lee
HOUGHTON MIFFLIN HARCOURT, 2005

The Maps of Tolkien's Middle-earth
Brian Sibley, John Howe, J. R. R. Tolkien
HOUGHTON MIFFLIN HARCOURT, 2003

Master of Middle-earth
Paul H. Kocher
RANDOM HOUSE, 2002

The Power of Tolkien's Prose
Steve Walker
PALGRAVE MACMILLAN, 2012

The Ring of Words: Tolkien and the Oxford English Dictionary
Gulliver, Marshall, Weiner
HARPERCOLLINS PUBLISHERS LTD, 1992

The Road to Middle-earth
Tom Shippey
MARINER BOOKS, 2003

The Tolkien Family Album
John Tolkien, Priscilla Tolkien
HARPER COLLINS PUBLISHERS LTD, 1992

Tolkien and the Great War
John Garth
MARINER BOOKS, 2005

Tolkien: Man and Myth
Joseph Pearce
HARPERCOLLINS PUBLISHERS LTD, 1999

Web sites

The American Tolkien Society
www.americantolkiensociety.org

The Hobbit movie news
www.the-hobbit-movie.com

Houghton Mifflin, US publisher
www.hmhbooks.com/features/lordoftheringstrilogy/

The Lord of the Rings movie
www.lordoftherings.net/home.htm

Marquette University Collection
www.marquette.edu/library/archives/tolkien.shtml

The Tolkien Estate
www.tolkienestate.com

The Tolkien Gateway
www.tolkiengateway.net/wiki/Main_Page

The Tolkien Library
www.tolkienlibrary.com

Unless otherwise stated, all quotes are from J. R. R. Tolkien. These are widely distributed on the Internet, but the key original sources are Humphrey Carpenter's *J. R. R. Tolkien, A Biography*, and *The Letters of J. R. R. Tolkien*.

Index

Acknowledgments

The publisher would like to thank the following individuals and organizations for their kind permission to reproduce the images in this book. Every effort has been made to acknowledge the pictures, and we apologize if there are any unintentional omissions.

AKG Images/British Library: 41; Ullstein Bild: 2, 13.
Alamy/AF archive: 75, 123TL, 123C; The Print Collector: 73B.
Mikhail Belomlinsky/Private Collection/The Bridgeman Art Library: 51T, 69C, 71C, 85C
Birmingham Archives: 21B, 25B, 27C.
JP Bowen: 39B.
Ernest Brooks/National Library of Scotland: 35B, 61BL.
Carcharoth: 12B.
Ceridwen: 119R.
From the private collection of Pieter Collier/www.tolkienlibrary.com: 16, 17, 49BL, 67T, 77C, 79BL, 81C, 97C, 99C, 102TR, 105C.
W.G. Collingwood: 33BR.
Corbis/Art By By Bill Petras/ZUMA Press: 145C; Seth Joel: 113B; TWPhoto: 133C.
Andrew Dunn/http://www.andrewdunnphoto.com: 43B.
Diacritica: 118TR, 155T.
Exet: 31T.
Flickr/Adam Simmons: 12T; Andy Mabbett: 23BC; Doc Searls: 43TR; hjjanisch: 15T, 129B; Joshua Eckert: 149C; phew_album: 143C; Tony Hisgett: 23BR; Will Merydith: 143C, 153R.
Fotolia: 13B, 23C, 24, 27TR, 47BR, 121TL; Alexey Kuznetsov: 56TR, 62; alexmillos: 143BR; ANK Design: 4, 114, 153C; Complot: 142; Creative HQ: 85, 106B; Dusan Kostic: 49BR; Florent Bhy: 6, 113TL, 152L; fxegs: 143B;

Hank Frentz: 45TR; Jaroslaw Brzychcy: 141T, 83BL; koya79: 40, 41BR; Les Cunliffe: 57TL; Paul Liu: 83BL, 106BR; Péter Mács: 145T; PiLensPhoto: 15C; Pshenichka: 121TR; radodn: 117C; Rafael Ben-Ari: 113TR, 152R; Sergej Khackimullin: 143; Sergej Razvodovskij: 29; Stephen Orsillo: 30; Stephen Orsillo: 31; Tom Bayer: 145BR; vadim yerofeyev: 150; Volker Haak: 11B.
Getty Images/AFP: 127B; Haywood Magee: 73T; Historic Map Works LLC and Osher Map Library: 14; Julian Love: 45TL; Time & Life Pictures: 43R.
http://www.ioniafilms.com/ Chris Bouchard: 139C.
Library of Congress: 11R, 21CR, 23BL, 29C, 29T, 35T, 39C, 41TL, 53BL, 59T, 61BC, 61BR, 103TL, 149TL.
Mary Evans Picture Library: 53C, 89L, 121B; Epic: 18, 25, 157T; INTERFOTO/Sammlung Rauch: 11T, 41BL.
Copyright Angus McBride, by kind permission of Pat McBride: 137BC, 137BL, 137BR.
NASA: 145B.
Oosoom: 12C.
Ozeye: 43L.
Tony Peters: 135L.
Photoshot/James Fisher: 131B.
© Copyright Billett Potter, Oxford: 47TR, 51C, 59B, 83C, 103C, 157B.
Rex Features: 10, 35R, 45BR, 139T; Adrian Sherratt: 119TL; CSU Archv/Everett: 115TR; Everett Collection: 117BR; Moviestore Collection: 77B, 77TL, 89R, 129C, 131T; New Line/Everett: 15, 79TR, 81T, 87B, 127C; Peter Brooker: 113TC; Simon Runting: 125C.
Shutterstock/3drenderings: 71CR; abracadabra: 92TR, 107BL; Alex Staroseltsev: 150; Algol: 97B, 107BR, 133L; andreiuc88: 99B, 157C; Anthro: 117CL; Antonio Abrignani: 80, 91C, 107C, 115C; Audrey Snider-Bell: 20TR, 60L; basel101658: 118B; benchart: 86; Betacam-SP: 97T;

BMP: 152C; Brocreative: 37T; Cattallina: 99T; catwalker: 120TR, 120TR; Clara: 93B; Convit: 33BL; createsima1: 58, 59C; David Crosbie: 95C; David Hughes: 149BL; Davor Pukljak: 100TR, 101BR; EhudBenPorat: 125B; ErmesS: 69R; Faraways: 124, 125R; Free Soul Production: 3, 95T; Georgios Kollidas: 115BR; Grimplet: 146 hamidisc: 76; Henrik Larsson: 73BR; IgorGolovnio: 21TR; IgorXIII: 69TR; Irina Ovchinnikova: 135T; J.D.S.: 136; jara3000: 44, 45BL; Jaroslaw Grudzinski: 95B; John David Bigl III: 90T, 106BL, 108T, 147T; JPL Designs: 27B, 60BR; Katrina Leigh: 91B; Kevin Eaves: 36; KSPhotography: 147BR; Lia Koltyrina: 93TL; Louella938: 74BR; Louella938: 75TR; Mark William Penny: 79BR; mtkang: 78; patrimonio designs limited: 7, 117TR; Pavel K: 135B; pavila: 102L; Peter Radacsi: 93C; photobank.kiev.ua: 119BR, 154BL; PhotoStocker: 88T; RestonImages: 141C, 153L; rook76: 126TR, 126TR, 133BC, 133C, 133C, 152T; Rozbyshaka: 77TR, 107B; s_bukley: 129TR; Sam Strickler: 85B; Sergey Mikhaylov: 39T; Slava Gerj: 13L; Smishonja: 95TL, 107BC; Styxe: 108B; Tadeusz Ibrom: 67C; Tamara Kulikova: 50; Thomas Pajot: 133BR; Valzan: 55BL; Vectomart: 132TR; wabbit photo: 71; WH Chow: 37C; Yangchao: 148.
Thinkstock: 72, 75T, 109, 141, 151T.
Topfoto: 101BL; National Pictures: 49TL, 105C, 110; Pamela Chandler/ArenaPAL/www.arenapal.com: 49TR, 55R, 57C, 64, 67B, 101C, 149BR; The Granger Collection, New York: 47BL; Topham Picturepoint: 87T, 151BR.
Emery Walker: 33TR.
Dana Wullenwaber: 135R.

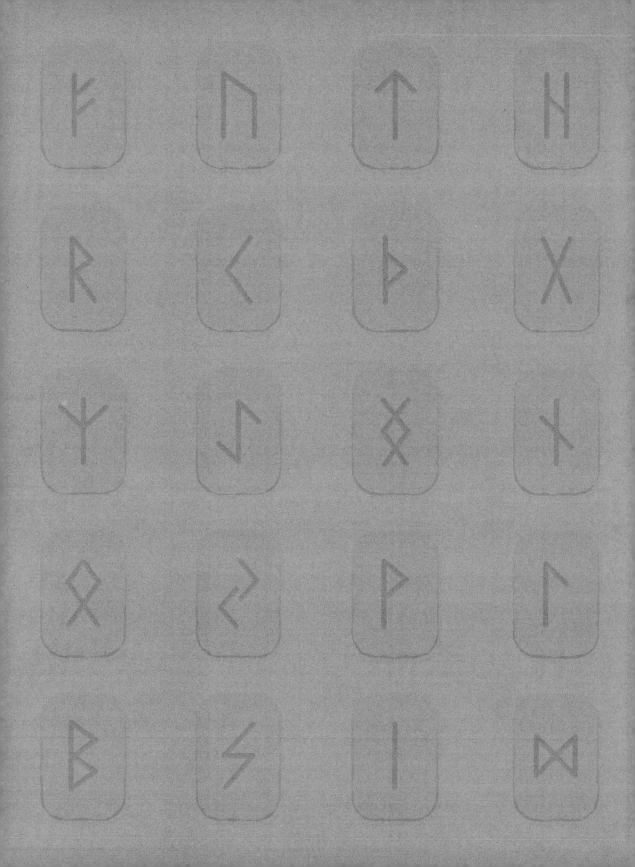